NED PRESS

ADAM TURL

GOTHIC CAPITALISM

ART EVICTED
FROM HEAVEN & EARTH

GOTHIC CAPITALISM
Adam Turl

First published by Revol Press 2025

Revol Press, Finland

Copyright © 2025 by Adam Turl

Print ISBN 978-952-65459-2-9 (softcover)
ebook ISBN 978-952-65459-3-6 (EPUB)

Design: Adam Turl
Cover: Adam Turl and Tish Turl, The Certainty of Math #3, mixed-media painting and collage (2024)

CONTENTS

For Tish, my rose du désert.

EVICTED FROM HEAVEN AND EARTH

Contemporary art — and culture more generally — has been progressively evicted from both Heaven and Earth. Art and culture have been divorced from a pre-modern promise of spiritual ascension or transcendence as well as the emancipatory impulses of modernity (Marxism, anarchism, and even bourgeois teleologies of progress). The avant-garde art model that often promised a revolutionary democratizing potential has become institutionalized and weak — detached from concerns and audiences that might otherwise revitalize it. We need to reorient avant-garde art production toward popular concerns, audiences and forms. Such a capacity, once dreamed of by avant-garde artists, has since been co-opted into a principally profit-driven global art scene. This book proposes we wrest art away from the dominant culture, using the art space as a theatrical, social and spiritual space that gives voice to proletarian narratives: the narratives of those who hold the power to abolish capitalism and create a genuine democratic society.

Art has a dual social-spiritual function that is threatened by the economies and ideologies of the art world, broader culture, and a faltering neoliberal patronage. Art faces a "crisis of substitutability"[1] — due to its replacement by digital social media and artificial intelligence. All this is fostered by the passivity of the neoliberal center, the growth of the far-right (which captures spaces of "belief" abandoned by the center and left). In this sense, art is evicted both from the material concerns of its historically critical avant-gardes, as well as the spiritual concerns of its cultic origins.

The proletarian subject experiences what I call a 'gothic-futurist' temporal displacement. The material convulsions of capital constantly create new spaces (and the promise of new spaces) for semi-autonomous social and cultural relations, only to tear them asunder. Each of these presents a trauma to the social unconscious — which itself

---

1 See Davis, Ben, *Art in the After-Culture* (Haymarket Books, 2022).

stretches from social infancy (the dawn of primitive communism) to the failures and horrors of the 20th and 21st centuries.[2] These failures have led to a simultaneously gothic and futurist progression of culture arising from an uneven and combined development (UCD). The term UCD was famously adopted by Leon Trotsky to explain how late Tsarist Russia combined both the most archaic social and economic forms as well as the most advanced.[3] UCD was initially seen as a phenomenon on the edges of capitalist development. In the neoliberal era, as industry became regionalized and globalized, UCD became visible in the capitalist core with deindustrialization and globalized labor markets. This appeared to "roll back time" in various rust-belts as uneven development could be seen in the contrast between dying industrial cities and the sleek promise of urban development and digital capitalism. In truth, UCD has always been central to capitalism.

This is the context in which the contemporary worker is becoming increasingly cybernetic. For our purposes here, "cybernetic" will refer, as it does in much of the academic literature on the subject, not only to the bodily fusion of human beings with technology but also the growing social and psychological fusion of individuals with technology and mass media, particularly digital media. If, in Marxist terminology, capital is dead labor — the wealth accumulated by the exploitation of previous generations of workers — and workers are living labor, we are increasingly fused with our ancestors, as dead workers. Despite the illusion that we might control the machines that characterize our era of production, those machines are shaped and determined by the needs of capital. As such they resist our every attempt.

The cybernetic worker embodies, in themselves, both the past and future. The past is horror and nostalgia. The future is both promise and

---

2 Turl, Adam, "A Thousand Lost Worlds: Notes on Gothic Marxism," *Red Wedge* (page no longer available, 2014).

3 Dunn, Bill and Radice, Hugo, eds., *100 Years of Permanent Revolution: Results and Prospects* (Pluto Press, 2006), 9.

threat. The present is precarity.

The word 'avant-garde' comes from the military term 'advanced guard' — meaning the elite soldiers who forged ahead and mapped new territory. That term was later applied to modernist artists of the early 20th century, who up-ended our understanding of culture as an elite form tending towards transcendentalism. The succession of different art movements, challenging previous artists and movements, was often described by art historians in Hegelian or Freudian terms. In modern art, conceptual, stylistic, and formal innovation could seem to parallel social progress. With art being co-opted we no longer have an avant-garde guiding us with its beacon. It is up to the working class to regain that potential in culture and to emerge from the uneven development of gothic capitalism.

1. A THOUSAND LOST WORLDS: NOTES ON GOTHIC MARXISM[4]

Kollontai's Gothic Bolshevism—Gothic America—
A Thousand Lost Worlds—Profane illumination—
A collective subconscious—Gothic Marxism and Epic
Theater—The Romantic Dialectic

KOLLONTAI'S GOTHIC BOLSHEVISM

Alexandra Kollontai was a prominent leader in the October 1917 Revolution in Russia. She was a member of the Bolshevik Central Committee and later helped lead the Workers' Opposition to the degeneration of the revolution. Kollontai, one of the first to support Vladimir Lenin's "April Theses" calling for the overthrow of the provisional government, was, before her ultimate capitulation to Stalin, consistently located on the far left of Russian Marxism. After the revolution, Kollontai was elected commissar of social welfare but left her post after joining the Workers' Opposition. After the defeat of the Workers' Opposition she helped spearhead the Zhenotdel, the women's department of the Russian government, formed in 1920. Kollontai and other Bolsheviks aimed to educate workers about liberalized divorce laws and create projects to collectivize child-care, housework, education and elder care. While the government supported the Zhenotdel (with varying degrees of enthusiasm among some male comrades) in the early days of the Soviet Union, there was little to no funding available for its projects. Post-revolutionary civil war and economic sanctions had crippled the Russian economy. All efforts had been pushed into defending the cities and major industrial areas. People were starving and manufacturing did not have sufficient inputs to function.

---

4 A version of this chapter originally appeared in Turl, Adam, "A Thousand Lost Worlds."

The New Economic Policy (NEP) aimed to reintroduce limited free market relations in order to jump start the Russian economy; giving peasants an incentive to send food to the urban workers who were starving to death at their machines. The NEP was partially successful in these terms, but it also became associated with a new breed of charlatan and opportunist—the "NEP-man." With the Russian aristocracy and bourgeoisie all but wiped out, a layer of opportunists arose, largely from the old Tsarist bureaucracy, seeking to find their way in the chaos. These layers would produce the cadres of the Stalinist machine that displaced the old revolutionary Bolsheviks in the late 1920s.

Eric Naiman, in his article "When a Communist Writes Gothic," offers the intriguing theory that Kollontai, also a writer of fiction, produced an essentially feminist allegory of the degeneration of the Russian Revolution in a gothic novella, *Vasilisa Malygina*. The novella tells the story "of a committed young Communist in the early 1920s" who "leaves her housing commune to visit her lover, now a factory director, in the provinces." Vasilisa discovers her lover has fallen prey to corruption and has taken on a mistress with bourgeois tastes. Vasilisa finds herself trapped in her lover's new mansion in a classic storyline (think of Alfred Hitchcock's *Rebecca*). The story begins, Naiman argues, as if it were a Russian propaganda novel, such as Nikolai Chernyshevsky's *What is To Be Done?* (the title later taken by Lenin for his classic pamphlet) but ends in "established Gothic lines." As in classic gothic novels, Vasilisa is stripped of her subjectivity and her modernity as the domestic patriarchal space (the mansion) and its (bourgeois and aristocratic) trappings consume her.[5]

Naiman interestingly draws a comparison to the subjective corruption of Vasilisa and the language Kollontai used to describe the degeneration of the Russian Revolution during her role as the spokesperson

---

5 Naiman, Eric, "When a Communist Writes Gothic: Aleksandra Kollontai and the Politics of Disgust," *Signs*, Vol. 22, No. 1 (Autumn, 1996), 3-4, 7, 10.

for the Workers' Opposition. The bourgeois specialists, the NEP-men, were described as "immigrants from the past." The opportunists were corrupting Soviet society with "an alien spirit" The "flesh of the flesh" of the working-class was corrupted. "The red blood corpuscles — the working class — are leaving us," leaving the Bolshevik party.[6]

Vasilisa is (almost) the paragon of communist virtue. She finds herself surrounded by an alien spirit, by "immigrants from the past." As Lenin himself argued, the NEP was a step backward (essentially re-animating the corpse of capitalism) so that the Bolsheviks could buy time. The NEP corruption, however, threatened the proletarian revolution itself. Vasilisa's mansion represented this decay: "This step backward into time, moreover, [that] might threaten to place the proletariat in the position earlier occupied by the bourgeoisie" — the creation of a gothic Bolshevism. After Stalin consolidated his power in 1929 all the gains of the October Revolution, of workers and women alike, were rolled back. Abortion and divorce were heavily restricted. The social role of women was curtailed. Kollontai lived out her days in diplomatic exile as ambassador (in Norway, Mexico and Sweden) while her former comrades were killed one by one in Stalin's dungeons.[7]

GOTHIC AMERICA

In Kerry James Marshall's painting, *Our Town* (1995), the artist presents a semi-abstracted and semi-corrupted idyllic image of the Great Society era. The painting depicts what looks like a 1960s promotional image of a housing project. Two Black children — riding a bike and running — are shown in the foreground. But the idealistic image is somewhat contrasted to the expressionistic use of paint applied to a canvas tarp. The hopes of the Great Society and the "War on Poverty" were dashed early — crashing against the reality of the Vietnam War. What hap-

---

6 Naiman, "When a Communist Writes Gothic," 13-15.
7 Naiman, "When a Communist Writes Gothic," 17.

pened to the poor would soon happen to women and the American working-class in the following decade.

Roe v. Wade (1973) turned out, in hindsight, to be a high point for the women's liberation movement. The Equal Rights Amendment (ERA) was defeated by a renewed right-wing onslaught. Middle-class feminist organizations progressively dropped demands that fused class and gender. Child-care, abortion funding, elder-care, and similar issues that were at the forefront of the radical phase of second wave feminism fell to the side as a narrow legalistic — now failed — defense of abortion became central. In the 1990s and 2000s it became the norm for leading feminists to point away from active struggles. Susan Faludi and Naomi Wolf decried "victim feminism" and counterposed it to so-called "power feminism" which focused on the psychology of a handful of rich and powerful women. The retreat to psychology mirrored the internal retreat of Kollontai's heroine. America's patriarchal mansion was badly damaged but remained intact.

In the 1970s other battles were waged — the battle of the left and the battle of the American industrial worker. The "New Left" that had been produced by the 1960s student and Black liberation struggles tried to gain a foothold in American society. Tens of thousands of radical activists aimed to build Leninist revolutionary groups (of different taxonomies) among American workers, in organizations such as the Communist Party, the Socialist Workers Party, the Workers World Party, the Progressive Labor Party, the Revolutionary Communist Party, Communist Party (Marxist-Leninist), the Communist Labor Party, and the International Socialists. Within a few decades, only one or two organizations would be of (modest) importance. Most of the revolutionary left crumbled into largely irrelevant sects.[8]

---

8 Since this was written the International Socialists has also fragmented, with their largest US group, the ISO collapsing after its leadership covered up a rape. The Democratic Socialists of America exploded in size and then began a decline; although it remains the largest organized socialist formation in the country. The most important

This process was related to the decline of the industrial working-class. The 1970s were a decade-long battle between the far left and the right for the the soul of American worker. Jefferson Cowie, in his book, *Stayin' Alive*, cites Gil Scott-Heron: "America doesn't know if it wants to be Matt Dillon or Bob Dylan." A truck driver, in 1968, put it more bluntly, remarking that he would either vote for the racist candidate George Wallace or the Communist Party.[9] As the liberal post-war consensus collapsed in the wake of Vietnam and Watergate, and under the pressures of the 1970s economic crisis, Cowie argued that the American working-class was being pulled in a thousand political directions. The 1970s were the decade of wildcat strikes in coalfields, in auto and steel plants, in the post-office and in trucking. The ultimate failure of the left, and success of the right, in capturing the imagination of white male industrial workers eased the U.S. neoliberal shift, ultimately deindustrializing and liquidating much of the industrial workforce.

A universe of cultural signs and artifacts was left behind as the Great Society, Women's Liberation, Black Liberation, the New Left and the New Deal working-class were dismantled. It took a few hundred years, but the United States finally became as gothic as its Old World, living in the defeats of liberation struggles and within the limits of tyrannical "realisms."

A THOUSAND LOST WORLDS

The point of analyzing this dynamic is that the "average" left-wing cultural producer can use it — to understand that mere didactic propaganda, while needed, is insufficient within the Janus-faced culture of contemporary capitalism. There are limits to what can be explained. There

left organization in the US was, after that, probably Socialist Alternative. That group, however, has also gone into decline and its most prominent member, Kshama Sawant, left the organization.

9 Cowie, Jefferson, *Staying Alive: The 1970s and the Last Days of the Working-Class* (New Press, 2010).

are limits to what can be communicated without the invocation of the gothic artifact. That artifact evokes worlds that can no longer exist—worlds that wither in the digital light. Its mythological quality is part and parcel of its weight — whether it is the mythology of a chivalrous medieval world or the mythologies of the bygone heyday of the industrial worker. It is not merely a false consciousness embodied in these myths and projections of meaning — it is genuine mourning for universes and people lost to ruthless novelty. It is an imagining of what was and what could have been, in a time and place when what one did might still have mattered. It is also, however, a frightening artifact — reminiscent of past tyrannies and the demise of then-contemporary worlds. It is the monster in the child's closet — alluring and horrible all at once.

There is much more exposition and unpacking to do on this question of a gothic dialectic in capitalist culture: What is gothic Capitalism? Of primary importance for us, in the United States, is the post-industrial ruin, the shells of the 1970s, when hopes for feminist, Leninist, Black Nationalist and working-class radicalism all crashed on the shoals of the neoliberal future. To let history wash over you is to be consumed by a past of horror and nostalgia, a history of autonomy gained and lost, repeatedly, and on various levels. Cultures (within capitalism) die every day, sublimated into new cultures, which in turn will die. Capital imagines the world after its own negation — but only in its dreams. Writ large, capital can only reproduce.

GOTHIC MARXISM

The initial impetus for the gothic in art and literature stemmed from the marginalization of medieval forms by bourgeois relations and industrialization. The gothic castle and the abbey stood in ruins, projecting both a nostalgia and fear of the past — things that were lost but also alien and threatening to modern life. The dynamics of capital continually recreate this process in contemporary culture, on various scales and in various geographies. This dynamic is the cultural echo of combined and uneven development. The hard-fought autonomy of the small businessman is destroyed as capital is consolidated in larger units. "Self-made men" are proletarianized — as (far fewer) proletarians become "self-made men." In the process thousands of little gothic worlds are created. The reign of the painter was supplanted by the photograph and film, which in turn have been supplanted by the digital image. Similarly, the American industrial worker has been expelled from the liberal-consumerist Eden of post-WW2 capitalism; and in the neoliberal wilderness has become aware of his or her nakedness. Capitalist technological change lays waste to trades, making people irrelevant unless they can carve a niche out as some kind of embodiment of nostalgia.

As for the class struggle, while partial victories are possible (however few and far between at a particular moment), as long as capital reigns, the history of bourgeois society is one of emancipatory dead-ends and cul-du-sacs. It is a history of post-Marxisms and post-feminisms, of academicized 'what-ifs?' More gothic worlds are born — in the shells of factories, in the empty union halls, in the empty mansions of declassed small capitalists, in the photographs of failed revolutions and in the broadsheets of all but forgotten sects. All of which co-exist alongside glossy alternatives that serve as castles on the hill: cryptocurrency, insta-fame, online political "commentary."

I first heard China Miéville use the phrase "gothic Marxism" in a talk on "Marxism and Halloween" at the Socialism 2013 conference in Chicago. Miéville invoked the concept in relationship to the idea of "solidarity with monsters," an impulse toward (or need for) solidarity with those that capitalist society has made monstrous by virtue of their inherent or voluntary opposition to the standardization of everyday life — the outliers in a system of generalized commodity production. Taken by this term, I Googled "gothic Marxism" and asked around. Margaret Cohen's 1994 book *Profane Illumination* seemed to be the main text explicitly dealing with the term. *Profane Illumination* focuses, in part, on the inter-war European cultural production and criticism of André

Breton and Walter Benjamin. As the word "gothic" implies, it concerns itself with the historical abortions and aberrations of a system based on constant innovation and constant destruction. Cohen provides the following rubric of Gothic Marxist concerns:

> (1) the valorization of the realm of a culture's ghosts and phantasms as a significant and rich field of social production rather than a mirage to be dispelled; (2) the valorization of a culture's detritus and trivia as well as its strange and marginal practices; (3) a notion of critique moving beyond logical argument and the binary opposition of a phantasmagorical staging more closely resembling psychoanalytic therapy, privileging nonrational forms of 'working through' and regulated by overdetermination rather than dialectics; (4) a dehierarchization of the epistemological privilege accorded the visual in the direction of that integration of the senses dreamed of by Marx in *The 1844 Manuscripts*.... and (5) a concomitant valorization of the sensuousness of the visual: the realm of visual experience is opened to other possibilities than the accomplishment and/or figuration of rational demonstration.[10]

While each of these points has its merits, my primary goal is to use the work of Cohen and others to sketch the existence of a gothic dialectic inherent in capitalist culture. It's a goal that Cohen does not necessarily share, as she seems to deny any causal relationship between base (economics) and superstructure (culture). Rather than counterposing overdetermination to dialectics, it is my assertion that a general Gothic dialectic is born of a series of cultural contradictions that echoes the structural contradictions of capitalist relations and production. That is to say, there is nothing inherently undialectical about

---

10 Cohen, Margaret, *Profane Illuminations* (University. of Chicago Press, 1995), 11-12.

the scientific concept of overdetermination. Overdetermination holds that effects can be a product of multiple and contradictory causes. For example, an evolutionary change in a species can be the product of several environmental and genetic shifts. In art and society, multiple contradictions find expression in the mediated cultural superstructure — the ideologies and norms that govern culture — filtered through the "collective dream" sketched by theorist Benjamin and writer Breton with their fusion of insights from Karl Marx and Sigmund Freud.

The material convulsions of capital constantly create new spaces (and the promise of new spaces) for semi-autonomous social and cultural relations — only to tear them asunder.[11] Each of these is a trauma to the social unconscious — which itself stretches from social infancy (the dawn of primitive communism) to the failures and horrors of the 20th and 21st centuries. The human social unconscious is replete with its own repressions, libidinal impulses and manifestations. However mediated and co-opted this cultural superstructure may be, its tectonics echo the movement and impact of capital as described by Karl Marx in the 19th century. While it is true that Marx was limited by the language and assumptions of that century (and while it is true that would-be Marxists have often misrepresented Marx in a mechanical and deterministic fashion) cultural autonomy is partial, contingent and in constant flux. This understanding cuts against both the vulgar Marxist tendency toward economism — or class reductionism — as well as postmodern and post-structuralist notions that cultural signs float unconnected to a material base.

PROFANE ILLUMINATION

The detritus of civilization — the historical debris of bourgeois society as it refracts capital into cultural objects and concepts — is the mandala of gothic Marxism. At the level of summary Cohen asserts that

---

11 One of the greatest recent examples is, of course, the utopian promises of the Internet itself.

gothic Marxism "charts the contours of a Marxist genealogy fascinated with the irrational aspects of social processes, a genealogy that both investigates how the irrational pervades existing society and dreams of using it to effect social change."[12] She opposes this to "vulgar Marxism," which, in her view, holds a deterministic and mechanical view of human development rooted in the Enlightenment.[13] While this is a somewhat reductive notion in itself — there were many Enlightenment thinkers who, like most of the early Romantics, rejected this deterministic notion of progress — it is true that vulgar Marxism (Stalinism and Social Democracy in particular) failed to connect to the spiritual condition of then-contemporary human beings. That ground was ceded to fascism. The human need for mythology was manipulated to obscure the condition of the exploited and oppressed and to direct spiritual energy into fascism. As Breton argued during WW2, there was a "vital necessity [for] a myth opposed to that of Odin."[14] Walter Benjamin argued that "the overcoming of religious illumination" resided in a "profane illumination, a materialist, anthropological inspiration."[15] This anthropological approach (which Benjamin also applied to Bertolt Brecht's theater) aimed to free Marxism from its supposed 19th century baggage (and 20th century distortions) by connecting it to the grand arc of human development.[16] This mining of the past, whether by Breton and the ghosts of Paris, or Benjamin's *Arcades Project*, aims to say something about the present that might not otherwise be articulated: "If images from the past spring to legibility in the present, it is because they speak to its concerns."[17] Benjamin argued:

---

12 Cohen, *Profane Illuminations*, 1-2.
13 Cohen, *Profane Illuminations*, 2-3.
14 Cited in Löwy, Michael, *Morning Star: Surrealism, Marxism, Anarchism, Situationism, Utopia* (University of Texas Press, 2009), 15.
15 Cohen, *Profane Illuminations*, 3.
16 Cohen, *Profane Illuminations*, 4-5.
17 Cohen, *Profane Illuminations*, 11.

> [W]e believe the charm they exert on us reveals that
> they still contain materials of vital importance to us
> — not, of course, for our architecture, the way iron
> truss-work anticipates our design; but they are vital
> for our perception, if you will, for the illumination of
> the situation.[18]

A COLLECTIVE SUBCONSCIOUS

Both Breton and Benjamin sought a fusion of Freud's insights with
a Marxist framework in order to navigate the mediated nether space
between base and superstructure, the gearing of the "psychoanalytic
account of the unconscious toward the forces of material determination at issue in Marxism."

> It is well known that Marx nowhere really divulged
> how the relationship between superstructure and in-
> frastructure should be conceived in individual cases.
> All that can be said with confidence is that he envi-
> sioned a series of mediations, as it were transmissions,
> interpolated between the material relationships of
> production and the remoter realms of the superstruc-
> ture, including art.[19]

As Cohen notes, Benjamin took aim at what he saw as the insufficiency
of Marxist criticism, "now swaggering, now scholastic," by exploring
this mediation. While Benjamin, unlike many of his would-be follow-
ers, never rejected the basics of Marxism and dialectical materialism,
this area of study led to accusations of "undialectical" thinking — in
particular from Adorno — implicitly or explicitly tied to Benjamin's
past Jewish mysticism. Benjamin argued that a wish-image arose from
this collective subconscious marked in "traces in thousands of config-

---

18 Cited in Cohen, *Profane Illuminations,* 15.
19 Cohen, *Profane Illuminations,* 15.

urations of life" — a constant revision of human subjectivity through a long historical process. Benjamin's role, the role of the critic, was to "awaken the world from the dream of itself" — a social outcome not dissimilar to the personal outcome of Freudian analysis. Such a privileged role assigned here to the critic is unfortunate. While this process is useful for understanding and producing art and culture, such an "awakening" did not in the end manifest via art, let alone art criticism. If anything, the modernist period has shown us that particular awakening is necessarily the product of wider social forces.

The detritus of capital is a marker of the dream: "The arcades and interiors, the exhibition and panoramas," that Benjamin famously walked and documented in Paris in the 1920s and 1930s for his *Arcades Project*. The ambiguity of the ruin is "dialectics at a standstill" — an elusive term that for Benjamin conjured a momentary intersection of past and present, a vision of utopia; or an exit from apocalyptic time. The wish images of capital create a kind of nostalgia at war with itself, a "striving for dissociation with the outmoded… These tendencies direct the imagistic imagination, which has been activated by the new, back to the primeval past." It is here that the libidinal impulse thrives in the collective subconscious. The wish images seek "both to sublate and transfigure the incompleteness of the social product and the deficiencies in the social order of production." In Breton's *Nadja* it may be Parisian ghosts. In the *Arcades Project* it is the 19th century salons, cafes, shops and promenades. In the 21st century there are yet more ghosts and ruins: from the industrial ruins of the 20th century to more recent antique memes, GeoCities pages, and the broken promises of cybernetic and neoliberal utopias.[20]

The origins of this mediated consciousness are bound up with the origin of human beings as a unique and distinctive species. Our cultural logic is still marked by social infancy and childhood. It was the Austrian

---

20 Cohen, *Profane Illuminations*, 15.

Marxist art critic Ernst Fischer who provided a materialist accounting for this "magic" in art — springing from a collective subconscious (although Fischer does not call it that). His argument about art's origins formed part of a Quixotic attempt to envisage the liberalization of eastern European cultural policies. In his 1959 text, *The Necessity of Art*, Fischer argues that art has a dual social-spiritual function because of its role in human evolution. He bases his account on the classic Friedrich Engels essay, "The Role of Labor in the Transition from Ape to Man" arguing, "art is almost as old as man [sic]. It is a form of work, and work is activity peculiar to mankind."[21] Human beings became human beings through the use of tools. The use of tools created an entirely different relationship between homo sapiens and the environment. This process altered the human mind, allowing for the emergence of spiritual belief and ritual. Our interaction with nature became mediated, and from that mediation came consciousness. This would also be the origin of Breton and Benjamin's social subconscious or unconscious.

The almost universal existence of shamanism in pre-class hunter-gatherer societies buttresses Fischer's explanation of art's magical origins. The South African archeologists David Lewis-Williams and Thomas Dowson were proponents of the idea that much cave painting had a shamanistic origin. Other anthropologists have embraced this interpretation of prehistoric art—experts such as Jean Clottes, the former research director at Chauvet Cave in France. Lewis-Williams based his research on firsthand observations of San Rock Art in South Africa and Clottes on his studies at Chauvet. The presence of phosphenes in the cave motifs — phosphenes are patterns and lines of light that appear in the eye that are not caused by the external light input — tend to confirm this analysis. As a product of mild hallucinations, they are evidence of a key aspect of shamanism — the practice of entering altered states of consciousness, visiting the "spirit world" or "underworld" and then bringing that narra-

---

21 Fischer, Ernst, *The Necessity of Art* (Verso, 2010), 24.

tive experience back to the group.

In its prehistoric formation, art was conceived as equal parts magic and science; realism and phantasmagoria; mythology and history. Even before human beings were divided into exploiter and exploited and oppressor and oppressed, art and culture were bound in a cosmic dream. While many of these elements — history and science for example — have become particular specializations within class society and capitalism's division of labor, art retains the mark of this dream. In capitalism, however, cultural dreams (and art) are usually commodities co-opted by capitalism. Breton's surrealists are a museum gift shop staple. Benjamin is a comedic meme archetype.

GOTHIC MARXISM AND EPIC THEATER

While Brecht's "Epic Theater," with its realist and didactic elements, does not confront the psychological aspects of a mediated mass subconscious as directly as Benjamin and Breton, Brecht deals with the same historical and anthropological concerns. The aim of Epic Theater was to emulate real life with slight absurd twists, bringing the audience in before jilting them with a question or thinking point. Its revolutionary aims were laid bare more than the poetically underscored works of say, Benjamin. Yet in terms of anthropological scale, Brecht looted the entire history of theater as well as history itself. As Stanley Mitchell argued:

> Epic theatre is a product of a historical imagination. Brecht's "plagiarism," his rewriting of Shakespeare and Marlowe, are experiments in whether a historical event and its literary treatment might be made to turn out differently or at least be viewed differently, if the processes of history are revalued. Brecht's drama is a deliberate unseating of the supremacy of tragedy and tragic inevitability. Echoing his own "Theses on the Philosophy of History," [Walter] Benjamin com-

ments: "It can happen this way, but it can also happen quite a different way — that is the fundamental attitude of one who writes for epic theatre."[22]

There is an obvious relationship between this final concept and Breton's confrontations with Parisian ghosts and Benjamin's interrogation of 19th century anachronisms. Brecht's use of history proper projected a geologic sense of time — not in terms of contradictions frozen in a dream, but in the pathos of proletarian morality.

> The pessimism [of Bertolt Brecht, Antonio Gramsci and Walter Benjamin] was strategic, designed to engender hope. Not for foreseeable victories or reversals of fortune, but for the survival of the species as such. This was not yet the nuclear age, but Brecht spoke prophetically: "They're planning for thirty thousand years ahead... They're out to destroy everything. Every living cell contracts under their blows... They cripple the baby in the mother's womb." In his friend, Benjamin discovered "a power that sprang from the depths of history no less deep than the power of the fascists" ... Brecht and Benjamin thought in millennia, geologically, of new dark and ice ages.[23]

THE ROMANTIC DIALECTIC

The gothic dialectic in capitalist culture is not separate from a material base. Like the Romantic dialectic, outlined by Michael Löwy, it comes from the inherent contradictions of broadly moving social phenomena. The Gothic and Romantic are closely linked. Both Breton and Freud based much of their interest in dreams on the Romantic tradition. The

---

22 Mitchell, Stanley, ed., Benjamin, Walter and Mitchell, Stanley, *Understanding Brecht* (Verso, 1977), xii.
23 Mitchell, *Understanding Brecht*, x.

echoes of a pre-capitalist past, in which qualitative value (in morality, aesthetics, philosophy, military skill) trumped quantitative value (mere holding of money) are bound up in the "magic" of the gothic object and the Romantic cultural impulse. As Löwy argues, Romanticism is often:

> ...reduced to a nineteenth century literary school, or a traditionalist reaction against the French Revolution — two propositions found in countless works by eminent specialists in literary history and the history of political thought. This is too simple... Romanticism is a form of sensibility nourishing all fields of culture... in opposition to the melancholic mood of despair, to the qualifying mind of the bourgeois universe, to commercial reification, to the platitudes of utilitarianism and above all, to the disenchantment of the world.[24]

Romanticism was, according to Löwy, the product of the contradiction between capitalism's celebration of individual personality on the one hand, and capitalism's debasement of that personality on the other. The late medieval/early capitalist intelligentsia found itself in material conflict with the utilitarian worldviews of the new ruling-class. As they were trained to see everything in terms of its qualitative value (good art, good philosophy, good ethics, good writing, etc.) the artists, poets, monks and philosophers of early capitalism bristled at how the new system valued everything by exchange. They looked back to an idealized pre-capitalist (sometimes pre-class) past. They counterposed 'spiritual' and 'humanistic' values against the 'rational' world capitalism claimed to be. They wrote against the "Dark Satanic Mills" of industry (Blake) and celebrated the night (Novalis) — because at night industry

---

24 Löwy, Michael, *Morning Star: Surrealism, Marxism, Anarchism, Situationism, Utopia* (University of Texas Press, 2009), 29.

ceased (or slowed) and the possibility of magic returned to the world.

Because an advanced and complex capitalism requires an intelligentsia that deals in qualitative as opposed to merely quantitative values, but at the same time sees these values as alien and hostile, capitalism continually recreates the conditions that first gave rise to late 18th century Romanticism. Löwy writes with Robert Sayre:

> Capitalism gives rise to independent individuals who can carry out socioeconomic functions; but when these individuals evolve into subjective individualities, exploring and developing their inner worlds and personal feelings, they enter into contradiction with a universe based on standardization and reification. And when they demand their imagination be given free play, they collide with the extreme mercantile platitude of the world produced by capitalist relations. In this respect, Romanticism represents the revolt of repressed, channeled, and deformed subjectivity and affectivity.[25]

The question for leftist artists today is: how do we take the contradictions borne of the individual artistic tendency while simultaneously collectivizing them to help develop critical and revolutionary impulses?

---

25 Löwy, Michael and Sayre, Robert, *Romanticism Against the Tide of Modernity* (Duke University Press, 2001), 25.

2. AGAINST THE WEAK AVANT-GARDE[26]

Boris Groys' Weak Avant-Garde—The Political
Economy of the Weak Avant-Garde—The Ideology
of the Weak Avant-Garde—Strong-Weak Images
vs. Weak Images—Weak Political Art (or
Situationism without Soviets)—The Commodification of the
Dematerialized—The Democratic Image—
The Gothic Cybernetic—Differentiated Totality, or the
Carnivalesque—The Art of Primitive Communism—
Cave Painting and Shamanism—The Anti-Shamans—
The Idolatry of Shadows

"Just their fingers' prints / staining the cold glass, is sufficient / for commerce, and a proper ruling on / humanity..." – Amiri Baraka, "The Politics of Rich Painters," 1964[27]

In the mid-1990s I saw an exhibit at the old Chicago Museum of Contemporary Art (MCA) of then-contemporary art from the former Soviet-Bloc nations of eastern Europe. The title of the show, *Beyond Belief* — curated by Laura Hoptman —announced a triumphant postmodernism. The artwork was presented as a post-mortem on the "God that failed." The work, however, was shaped by contradictory relationships to actual political failures, revolutions, national oppressions and tyranny. The conceptually pugilistic Czech artist David Černý exhibited a sculpture of a giant human baby with retail bar code for a face. Černý's *Babies* (1994-) have been installed in multiple locations over the years. At one point they were attached to Prague's famous Žižkov Televi-

---

26 This section draws on research from my 2016 written MFA thesis ("Towards an Evicted Avant-Garde," Sam Fox School of Design and Visual Arts/Washington University in St. Louis), and a series of articles that appeared in *Red Wedge Magazine* from 2015 to 2020, in *Imago*, and on the *Imago* website in 2022 — edited and reworked with new material from 2023.

27 Baraka, Amiri, *SOS: Poems 1961-2013* (Grove Press, 2014), 71.

sion Tower. The installation, *News from Dracula* (1994), by the Romanian art collective sub-REAL, combined a gymnastics pummel horse with, among other things, wooden stakes. Many of the artists in *Beyond Belief* did not so much reject narratives as seek to create new myths and stories out of the contradictory signs bequeathed by the collapse of "communism" and their sudden confrontation with neoliberal capital. The work, even if it wanted to, did not stand outside of history.[28] As Marek Bartelik notes in *Artforum*, the artists were "in many ways 'products' of the old system," and "reflect[ed] the collision of old values and those created by the free-market economy and democratization."[29]

While conceptual art in the "west" (particularly the United States) tended to focus on the definition of signs (and was therefore preoccupied with text), conceptual art in the Stalinist Block tended to focus on story and narrative. Eastern European conceptual art echoed Moscow conceptualism in this regard.[30] Conceptual art in Moscow came into being in a different and totalitarian context. It drew on Russian and Soviet literary traditions.[31] If conceptualism in the west was driven toward categorization and definition, Moscow conceptualism was driven by a sort of "graphomania" (a compulsion to write).[32] The targets of Moscow conceptualism were not the market or the commodification of culture; rather, as Boris Groys argues, they were the "rules of the symbolic economy that governed the Soviet Union in general."[33] This narrative conceptualism was connected to the way "normal" life functioned in

---

28 See the show catalog, Hoptman, Laura, *Beyond Belief: Contemporary Art from East-Central Europe* (Chicago Museum of Contemporary Art, 1995).
29 Bartelik, Marek, "Review: Beyond Belief," *Artforum* Vol 35, No 7 (March 1997), 97.
30 This passage is partly from Turl, Adam, "Interrupting Disbelief: Narrative Conceptualism and Anti-Capitalist Studio Art," *Red Wedge Magazine* (February 8, 2015).
31 Corris, Michael, "Total Engagement: Moscow Conceptual Art: Schirn Kunsthalle, Frankfurt," *Art Monthly* Issue 319 (September, 2008), 18-20.
32 Schlegal, Amy Ingrid, "The Kabakov Phenomenon," *Art Journal*, Vol. 58 No. 4 (Winter, 1999), 99.
33 Corris, "Total Engagement," 18-20.

the USSR. As Ilya Kabakov recalls, "[l]ife consisted of two layers, each person was a schizophrenic. Any person — a factory worker, intellectual, artist — had a split personality."[34]

Bulgarian artist Nedko Solakov made this double-life the subject of his confessional installation/sculpture *Top Secret* (1990) included in *Beyond Belief*: "[A] chest-file contains in alphabetical order notes arranged in alphabetical order with texts, drawings, and small objects that recount … the life of the author and about the period between 1976 and 1983, when, as a student who believed in Socialism, he collaborated with the secret service of the former political regime in Bulgaria."[35]

In most former Stalinist European states, the records of the secret police have been (at least partially) made public. Bulgaria is — or at least was at the time — an exception so there was little verifiable information about the extent of Solakov's collaboration. Regardless, his confession produced some controversy. Putting aside, for a moment, questions about Solakov's complicity in a totalitarian state capitalist regime, what is most striking is the translation of crude oppressive state data into subjectivities; a symbolic restoration of what was lost. The victims of the secret police are given the dramatic value of multiple hand-made, individual, subjective and expressive drawings.[36]

As almost everyone now agrees, post-modernism is gone, if not as a period of time, as a useful theoretical construct. The artists of the west, surrounded by economic decline, torrents of racism and sexism and ongoing imperial wars, can no longer pretend that history has ended. And yet, disbelief persists. Disbelief produces the transparent gestures of Damien Hirst, Jeff Koons, James Franco, Jay Z and Marina

34 Vidokle, Anton, "In Conversation with Ilya and Emilia Kabakov," *e-flux*, 40 (December, 2012).

35 Mihaylova, Vladiya, "Nedko Solakov and the Rest of the World" *Flash Art* 43 (January February 2010), 72.

36 Christov-Bakargiev, Carolyn, Lange, Christy, and Boubnova, Iara, *Nedko Solakov: All in Order, with Exceptions* (Hatje Cantz, 2011), 19.

Abramović.

While Solakov's confession intervenes directly at the intersection of the social and subjective, the collective and the spiritual, Abramović's 2011 "performance" at a gala fundraiser for the Museum of Contemporary Art (MOCA) in Los Angeles actively flattened human subjectivity. Actors were placed on "lazy susans" in the middle of dining tables. Only their heads appeared on the tables. They would rotate, "making eye contact with the donors/diners" that surrounded them. The actors were not allowed to respond to the actions of the guests or go to the bathroom. This included the possibility of being "fondled under the table." The choreographer Yvone Rainer argued that this "performance" recalled Pier Paolo Pasolini's 1975 film, *Salo,* about the "sadism and sexual abuse of a group of adolescents at the hands of a bunch of post-war fascists." Rainer continues:

> Reluctant as I am to dignify Abramović by mentioning Pasolini in the same breath, the latter at least had a socially credible justification tied to the cause of anti-fascism. Abramović and MOCA have no such credibility, only a flimsy personal rationale about eye contact. Subjecting her performers to public humiliation at the hands of a bunch of frolicking donors is yet another example of the Museum's callousness and greed and Ms. Abramovic's obliviousness to differences in context and some of the implications of transposing her own powerful performances to the bodies of others. An exhibition is one thing — this is not a critique of Abramović's work in general — but titillation for wealthy donor/diners as a means of raising money is another.[37]

---

37 Rainer, Yvonne, "Yvonne Rainer Blasts Marina Abramović and MOCA LA," *The Performance Club* (November 11, 2011): https://theperformanceclub.org/yvonne-rainer-blasts-marina-abramovic-and-moca-la.

Our contemporary art world produces Instagram traps and Meow Wolf spectacles, NFTs, AI generated images of apocalypse — while often, for example, silencing artists who have defended, even in mild terms, national rights of the Palestinians.

There are (or have been until very recently) three main overlapping arenas for institutional contemporary art: the established art market, the academic avant-garde and the canonical art museum. The artist's relationship to these is largely defined by petit-bourgeois commodity production and academic research; each of which are now threatened in various ways by the logic of capitalism's new digital technologies.

The poverty of meaning and political potential in contemporary art is structural and linked to wider economic and class-based concerns. The middle-class production of the art market is polarized between highly successful so-called "art entrepreneurs" and a mass of "dark matter" — tens of thousands of working-artists who cannot even dream of making a living at their craft but whose production is central to the maintenance of the art world. Indeed, many of these people may exist completely outside the art world proper.[38] Some of them are working-class in their "day jobs" and impoverished. The academic avant-garde is characterized, economically and socially, by a (sometimes proletarian) relationship to austerity in higher education, a highly rarefied and individualized relationship to academic rites (tenure, publishing, influence), and the inheritance of the avant-garde mantle.

The artist is always on the make; trying to become in materiality what they already believe themselves to be in essence — precisely, *artist.* There is no guarantee of patronage. And, since the end of the modernist avant-gardes, there is no longer an accepted coherence to what art is, what artists are, or an accepted debate over the nature of art. The artist is therefore trapped between the rigidity of their social

---

38 Sholette, Gregory, *Dark Matter: Art and Politics in the Age of Enterprise Culture* (New York: Pluto, 2011).

position and the supposed fluidity and openness of the contemporary art object or gesture. Within that trap are the often-unspoken things that the work cannot be: too didactic, earnest or confrontational. The academic avant-garde can scoff at the commodity status of the art object, jealously and rightly guarding tenure (its own commodity status), while tending to avoid the fact that the untenured artist must sell their work in order to eat. Contemporary art — at least for artists from more working-class backgrounds — suffers an unbearable lightness of being and an unbearable weight of becoming.

We have reached the Hegelian endgame; the fusion of art and philosophy. Not quite, as Arthur Danto notes, a negation of art by philosophy but their mutual collapse.[39] The art object has become, it is claimed, a philosophical argument. But it is a *Twilight Zone* ending for art history, modernism and the avant-garde. The zeros of painting, Kazimir Malevich's *Black Square* and Robert Rauschenberg's *White Paintings*, were long ago achieved. Malevich, with his canvases comprising only flat monochrome planes, created simple geometric fields and shapes that were imbued with a futurist cosmism.[40] Rauschenberg's *White Paintings*, produced a few decades later in the postwar American boom, were white canvases displayed to capture the shadows of the patrons who viewed them. Similar to the Buddhist-inspired conceptual musician John Cage, this was meant to provoke a meditative condition in the viewer, and expand, in a democratic manner, the possible content of the art gesture. In John Cage's *4'33"*, a piano player sits at a piano and plays no music. The atmospheric noises of the concert hall — and the coughs and movement of the audience itself — *become* the music.

In contemporary art, the *meaning* of these historic avant-garde gestures is often lost in favor of a weak version of their form.

---

39 Danto, Arthur, *Unnatural Wonders*, (New York: Colombia University Press, 2007), 10-13.
40 This dovetailed at the time with the utopianism of the early Soviet Union and was influenced by the esoteric philosophy of Cosmism.

Similarly, Echoing Joseph Beuys' "famous axiom" that "everyone is an artist," in contemporary art, *anything* can be made into art.[41] Beuys' autobiographical mythology included an apocryphal story about being rescued by nomadic Tartars after being shot-down in WW2. Beuys was a German bombardier. He claimed to have been wrapped in felt and fat by the Tartars. These materials figured prominently in his artwork. Perhaps sensing the problematics of the German Romantic artistic tradition after Nazism, Beuys tried to radically democratize the romantic impulse. As if to say, "yes, I am a special shaman mystic. But so is everyone else!" And Beuys took steps to prove that democratic impulse in action. For example, he allowed open enrollment in his classes — to the displeasure of his employer — while he taught at the Kunstakademie Düsseldorf. This aspect of his work, both personal and in connection to the wider Fluxus art movement, was related to what he called "social sculpture." Yet despite such efforts, which were not unique among the historic European artistic avant-garde, the world beyond the philosophical-art object remains stratified, full of prosaic wars, bigotries, and privations. As with Cage's music, Beuys' axiom was meant to expand the realm of what could be considered a philosophical art-object, and *who* might wield it. Beuys' performances and manipulations of found objects were meant to take the Duchampian 'readymade' art object — Marcel Duchamp famously exhibited objects such as an upturned urinal as an artwork, for example — and turn the readymade into a kind of poetic language. Decades later, readymades are central to a booming contemporary art economy that is seen as investment for its collectors. For example, Maurizio Cattelan's *Comedian* (2019) — literally a banana duct taped to a wall — was recently auctioned by Sotheby's for more than six million dollars.

This is not to say that Beuys had entirely "good" politics. Despite

---

41 Groys, Boris "The Weak Universalism," *e-flux* 15, April 2010: http://www.e-flux.com/journal/the-weak-universalism.

his personal antipathies to racism, he sometimes reproduced national essentialism in his work. In *I Like America and America Likes Me*, the United States is represented by both a coyote (as a symbol of Native American culture) and a stack of *Wall Street Journals* (as a symbol of post-war American capitalism). Likewise, Beuys celebrated Mahatma Gandhi with little understanding of Gandhi's caste bigotries, his sexism, his historic racism against Black Africans, or his role in holding back the class struggle in India.

Regardless, the radical aspect of the Beuysian democratic-romantic gesture is absent in much contemporary art. Yes, anything can be made into art. But there is a small army of theorists dedicated to parsing out what is and isn't art. Anyone can be an artist – if they are rich or solidly middle-class, or if they aren't too attached to the idea of eating dinner. A banana can be sold as art for millions of dollars. But it was purchased from a vendor moments before the auction for about forty cents. That vendor, Shah Alam, an impoverished immigrant from Bangladesh in his seventies, reportedly wept when he heard the banana had been resold for millions.[42]

In the context of neoliberal capitalism, the destruction of "art" as a specific category leaves art with commerce as its *raison d'etre*. In *K-Punk,* a posthumously published collection of online polemics and writings, Mark Fisher takes note of the empty faux realism and anti-sensualism of Tracy Emin's *Bed* installation at the Tate in 1998. Emin simply placed her bed in the museum. This looks, superficially, like a Duchampian readymade. It seems to imitate Beuys. But it really shows the "vacuity of her own preferences."[43] Beuys and Duchamp made an argument with their work. Duchamp argued for the expansion of art to include — as he joked — "American plumbing." Beuys argued that society *should* allow everyone to be an artist — not that phantasma-

---

42 Griffin, Allie, "NYC fruit vendor, 74, who sold banana devastated after it became viral $6.2M artwork: 'I am a poor man'," *New York Post* (November 28, 2024).
43 Fisher, Mark, *K-Punk* (London: Repeater, 2018), 276.

gorically everyone already was an artist. There is, notably, something seductive about the form and content of Duchamp's readymade urinal. There is something sensual about Beuysian fat and felt. But there is nothing seductive in *Bed*. Emin's antipathy to seduction and the sensual is — whatever her intent — ultimately bourgeois. It ratifies labor's alienation from the sensual.[44] This is art as *tautophrase*. A tautophrase is a colloquialism that is designed to short-circuit critical thinking — such as "boys will be boys," "a man's got to do what a man's got to do," or "if you know, you know." What Emin actually says (in this case) is: "it is what it is."

Art and philosophy have fused in the absence of social revolution. The result is a philosophical-art object that is profoundly weak. If the present model of serious contemporary art is a *weak avant-garde that reifies art's potential and further commodifies it*, the solution would appear to be a *popular avant-garde*: a rapprochement between artistic experimentation (*as art*) and mass emancipatory politics.

BORIS GROYS' WEAK AVANT-GARDE

In his 2010 essay, "The Weak Universalism," art critic and theorist Boris Groys points to some of these contradictions. Groys observes an "academicized late avant-garde" defined by its conditioning in art schools. Whereas the pre-avant-garde academy was focused on technical skill, according to Groys the weak avant-garde is defined by its knowledge of and exposure to the avant-garde cannon. Here the "deprofessionalization" of art, a product of democratic modernist gestures, becomes professional.

This weak avant-garde tends to produce weak visual signs. Like Emin's *Bed*, many of the paintings surveyed in the Museum of Modern Art's 2014 *Forever Now: Contemporary Painting in an Atemporal World* exhibition perform gestures of 20th century abstraction without their his-

---

44 See Marx, Karl, *The Economic and Philosophic Manuscripts of 1844* (Dover, 2007).

toric conceptual meaning and pathos. Two of the best artists included in the survey — Julie Mehretu and Oscar Murillo — use those tools to discuss (visually) an approach to the contemporary messianic moment (using Groys' terms). Mehrutu's paintings reproduce a complex interlocking of forms and movement that visually pivot from something like systems theory and rhizomatic networks.[45] They are beautiful paintings that encapsulate the movement of both globalization and computer networks. Murillo's stitched together abstracted fragments comment, in part, on the fragmented subjectivity of present-day life. In *Forever Now* some of these works were exhibited in heaps on the floor. But both Murillo and Mehretu's work seem to eschew a criticality, an argument for either art or subject. Mehrutu's work — while sometimes titularly evoking history — was easily incorporated into the lobby of Goldman Sachs' New York offices. This is because the work is, while more seductive than Emin's work, also something of a tautophrase. However important these themes are, the circulation of forms, finance, memes, persons, or capital is represented but not critiqued. Nor does the work telegraph a utopian, cosmic, or post-capitalist endgame. It simply *is*. Oscar Murillo's franken-paintings are similarly full of expressive pathos — in contrast to much of the work included in *Forever Now*. But they also struggle to articulate beyond the tautological. They incorporate subjective feelings far more than most of the popular abstraction that surfaced in the 2010s under the monikers "casualism" or "zombie formalism"— easy to understand paintings for a swollen art-collector class. Murillo's franken-paintings want to become both fragments and totalities. It is the latter that is elusive.

The basis of this kind of weakness, for Groys, is in the constant change and churning novelty of modern life. "[K]knowledge of the end of the world as we know it," Groys writes, "of contracting time, of the scarcity of time in which we live" produces a kind of "mes-

---

45 Groys, "The Weak Universalism."

sianic knowledge." The avant-garde becomes, according to Groys, "a secularized apostle… who brings to the world the message that time is contracting, that there is a scarcity of time." Because we live in a "chronically messianic" or "apocalyptic" epoch in which "change is the status quo," or "permanent change… our only constant," the visual artist seeks intentionally weak visual signs. These weak signs are the artists' attempt to produce "transtemporal" works of art; "art for all time."[46] Strong images and strong politics, it is implied, place a temporal mark within artworks. Groys describes the images of classical art, renaissance art, and popular culture as strong. Michelangelo's *Pieta* (1498-1499), a sculpture that depicts the dead Christ in his mother's arms, connects birth and death in a singular pathos. But strong images also echo beyond temporal constraint. The pieta, for example, has been quoted in dozens of films. In *Star Trek: The Wrath of Khan* (1982), Scotty, the chief engineer of the *Enterprise*, brings his dead nephew to the bridge of the starship in a scene reminiscent of the pieta.

It is hard to abstractly define a strong or weak image. It is not an essentialized category but a relationship to signification, social being, and time. In the present, strong images often become clichés and tropes, separated from their original meanings; usually in mass arts like film and television. But the use of strong images — a cross, a hammer and sickle, a raised fist, Islamic calligraphy — is often discouraged in art schools. The producers of weak images, trained in the art schools, seek to avoid clichés and contribute to a narrow 'discourse.'

Groys turns reification — or 'de-spiriting' in either the Marxist or classical philosophical sense — on its head. Instead of the subject being presented as an object (see György Lukács) —or the concrete being made abstract — due to the material interests (real or perceived) of bourgeois thinkers and artists, the concrete is made abstract to escape the temporal (but strong) images of a constantly changing popular cul-

46 Groys, "The Weak Universalism."

ture.[47] For Groys, Malevich's *Black Square* is the ultimate weak sign. The "transcendent images" in the "Kantian sense" (of an idealism outside of time) are not just products of artists' weak messianism but also invocations of a "weak universalism." The gods and utopias that animated the past have, in themselves, become weak. These weak images are to be contrasted, in Groys view, with "strong images with a high level of visibility" like "images of classical art or mass culture."[48]

While Groys offers many insights, most importantly the idea of the weak avant-garde itself, there are problems with his analysis. He glosses over the material basis of the weak-avant-garde and is selective in his genealogy of modernism. To make the case, for example, that the modernist avant-gardes always tended toward *weak* images one must restrict history to the visual arts (leaving aside cinema, literature, theater, poetry, music, etc.), and even then, one must excise Dada, surrealism, and the "stronger" images of expressionism, constructivism, futurism, etc. The avant-gardes of theater (see Bertolt Brecht) and film (see Sergei Eisenstein or Pier Paolo Pasolini) continued to embrace strong images (or strong-weak images). This all makes sense in Groys' schema but it leaves out a significant part of modern art history (often those elements most associated with emancipatory impulses).

THE POLITICAL ECONOMY OF THE WEAK AVANT-GARDE

There is a material basis for the weak avant-garde, both in the economy of the art world itself and the broader cultural dynamics of capitalism. The art world rests on three institutional pillars: the academic, the non-profit/museum art space, and the art market. A fourth "invisible" pillar supports the art world *as a world*: the army of art volunteers and unknown artists that comprise the "dark matter" of contemporary art.

47 I am using the term reification here in a mostly Lukacsian sense, informed by a left Romanticism — the abstraction of concrete social relations, the alienation of work and labor, and the thingification of the "life-world."
48 Groys, "The Weak Universalism."

These are the working-class artists that achieve no notoriety, the volunteers at community art centers, etc.[49] The art economy is largely one of individual producers who make art on speculation to be sold in a boutique market.[50] The vast majority of artists who participate are unable to "make ends meet" by art sales alone. Regardless, the demands of this market, oriented primarily toward wealthier collectors, tend to shape the artworks sold. See, for example, the almost assembly-line, art-by-the-foot production of Damien Hirst's dot paintings. Here is a possible explanation for "weak" images that Groys has missed — a prosaic truth that much of the bourgeoisie does not want challenging images hanging over their couches.

The logic of the market, of course, extends into the academic and non-profit art institution. In a 2016 survey of a thousand artists about compensation at non-profit US art spaces, "58.4 percent were completely unpaid, without even expense reimbursement. Even some of the largest institutions got low marks: New York's Metropolitan Museum of Art, for instance, has a total annual operating budget of more than $250 million but paid surveyed artists for only 14.3 percent of exhibitions."[51] In 1973 Holis Frampton wrote a letter to MoMA citing the case of post-war surrealist filmmaker Maya Deren, who, despite her "art world" notability, had starved to death in New York City.[52] As *Red Wedge* observes:

> After more than three-decades of accelerating government cutbacks, nonprofits now increasingly operate by the logic of capital accumulation in their own operations. Universities increase tuition and sacrifice

49 Sholette, *Dark Matter*, 1.
50 See Davis, Ben, *9.5 Theses on Art and Class* (Haymarket Books, 2013).
51 Ladendorf, Tom, "The Group of Artists That's Winning Fair Pay by Targeting Nonprofits," *In These Times*, January 26, 2016: http://inthesetimes.com/article/18764/wages-for-arts-sake.
52 Davis, Ben, *9.5 Theses on Art and Class*, 21-22.

education and research budgets for shiny new buildings. Museums sacrifice exhibition budgets for unnecessary expansions. Community groups increase the number of 'gatekeepers' to urgently needed (but dwindling) resources… As Lillian Lewis and Sara Wilson McKay observe in their article, 'Seeking Policies for Cultural Democracy: Examining the Past, Present and Future of U.S. Nonprofit Arts,' non-profits have been forced to increasingly rely on 'earned income' to maintain their operations.[53]

THE IDEOLOGY OF THE WEAK AVANT-GARDE

There is, however, an ideological factor beyond the market. As Danica Radoshevich argues in her essay, "Zombie Gallery? The German Ideology and the White Cube," "the bourgeois intellectual appeals to the abstract because he conceives of himself as in touch with some generalized unreservedly 'true' human condition." The status of the museum/non-profit space, and the academic cannon itself, is the echo of this bourgeois conceit. "When this [art] is installed in an empty, white walled gallery space," Radoshevich writes, "its supposed 'autonomy' and 'universal validity' is visually and materially heightened, while its relationships to social or material contexts is erased."[54] A clear example of this is when pre-modern works are placed into the white cube. A pre-modern African mask meant to be used in a ceremony is hung on a white wall. It floats there, no longer able to communicate its cosmic or social meanings via its situation or performative context. El Greco's *Assumption of the Virgin* (1577-1579) is displayed as a faux altarpiece at the

53 Editorial (Turl, Adam and Billet, Alexander), "Art in (Corporate) America," *Red Wedge*, (June 1, 2014).
54 Radoschevich, Danica, "Zombie Gallery? The German Ideology and the White Cube," *Red Wedge* (February 8, 2015): http://www.redwedgemagazine.com/commentary/the-white-cube-and-the-german-ideology-gallery-space-as-bourgeois-farce?rq=-zombie%20gallery.

Art Institute of Chicago. Instead of being a devotional object/image, it now *imitates* a devotional object/image. The contradiction of the "white cube" is that it both removes social content and elevates the objects placed within them. It therefore *changes* their meaning. The social-spiritual object becomes evidence of individual genius or a mapping and archiving of the other.

Postmodernism claimed to challenge canonical thinking. Postmodernism is a confusing set of concepts that came to prominence in the American academy in the 1980s, based in large part on the work of a certain layer of French intellectuals. These theories still inform, despite being largely discredited or discarded, a good deal of art curation. While the content of postmodernism is itself contradictory, it tended to emphasize a rupture between sign (image, text, word) and referent (the thing being represented). Some theorists saw postmodernism as a condition arising from "late capitalism" (see Frederic Jameson) while others saw it as a product of "modernity" more generally (see Jean Baudrillard). Other postmodernists argued that reason — or "scientific ways of knowing" — had become impossible and were ultimately based on irrationality anyway (see Jean Francois Lyotard). Nothing could truly be known beyond its immediacy. It was, in a sense, a philosophy of tautologies.

Contrary to its claims, postmodernism *reinforced* canonical thinking in the arts. Without generalization and engagement with some kind of historic subject, all that was left was a seemingly random genealogy. Postmodernism and post-structuralism, heralding the end of totalizing metanarratives (such as Marxism), promised liberation from the ideological constraints of the past. While in some cases spurring liberation from essentialist notions of identity, postmodernism emphasized a "discursive" notion of power, privileging not social movements of the exploited and oppressed but instead valorizing the theorist and professor. Fredric Jameson, David Harvey and Ben Davis were right: post-modernism was the cultural logic and ideology of neoliberal capital.[55] It celebrated social and cultural fragmentation at the very moment large corporations reorganized global finance, production and capital accumulation. An overgrowth of "anti-ideological" theory concealed a thousand real world disasters, or disasters in the making.

Jean Baudrillard famously wrote that the 1991 Gulf War didn't so much happen as it was an event on CNN. Meanwhile, the United States killed tens of thousands of retreating Iraqi soldiers on "The Highway of Death" and irradiated Iraq with depleted uranium. Quite clearly this war happened, and postmodern theory provided an alibi. As "totalizing metanarratives" were deemed reductive, globalization shifted trade and production networks to minimize environmental regulations, remove protections for indigenous persons, and destroy trade unions. As cybernetic utopianism was promoted with an almost ecclesiastical certainty, climate catastrophe slouched towards its increasingly present denouement. As the post-structuralists tutored a generation to be suspicious of Marxism, the aforementioned digital networks were enclosed by large capitalist firms — Microsoft, Amazon, Alphabet/Google, Meta/Facebook, Apple, Oracle, Adobe. The North American Free Trade Agreement (NAFTA) pushed millions of Mexican farmers off their land — by rewriting the Mexican constitution — while destroying hundreds of thousands of union manufacturing jobs in the U.S. The high-tech jobs of the future were sold — by President Clinton and others — as a coming solution. Those jobs never appeared in Mexican ejidos and Ohio factory towns. This doesn't even begin to discuss the so-called "War on Terror," the 2008 financial crisis, the rebirth of far-right populism and fascism in Europe and the US, Brexit, President Trump, fascism in India, racist police murders, the COVID-19 pandemic, and so on.

These unfolding disasters, recalling Walter Benjamin's "angel of history," are the material basis for the "state of permanent change"

55 See Davis, Ben, "The Age of Semi-Post-Post-Modernism," *Artnet* (2016): http://www.artnet.com/magazineus/reviews/davis/semi-post-postmodernism5-15-10.asp.

that Groys describes empirically. In Benjamin's "Theses on History," he cuts against the deterministic and vulgar passivity of both Stalinist and Social Democratic Marxists. That vulgar passivity was rooted in the idea of teleological progress — that "society" was, more or less, on a "one way street" toward a more rational, equal, scientific, and democratic future. Benjamin, trying to raise the alarm at the midnight of the last century (WW2, the Holocaust), attempted to salvage Marxism from this false understanding of history. Meditating on a painting by Paul Klee, he writes:

> There is a painting by Klee called *Angelus Novus*. An angel is depicted there who looks as though he were about to distance himself from something which he is staring at. His eyes are opened wide, his mouth stands open and his wings are outstretched. The Angel of History must look just so. His face is turned towards the past. Where *we* see the appearance of a chain of events, *he* sees one single catastrophe, which unceasingly piles rubble on top of rubble and hurls it before his feet. He would like to pause for a moment so fair, to awaken the dead and to piece together what has been smashed. But a storm is blowing from Paradise, it has caught itself up in his wings and is so strong that the Angel can no longer close them. The storm drives him irresistibly into the future, to which his back is turned, while the rubble-heap before him grows sky-high. That which we call progress, is *this* storm.[56]

The more sophisticated postmodernists would agree with Benjamin on the chaotic nature of history but disagree with Benjamin's solution — his description of revolution as "pulling the emergency

---

56 Benjamin, Walter, "On the Concept of History" (1940), version at https://www.marxists.org/reference/archive/benjamin/1940/history.htm.

brake" on social disaster. Sophisticated or not, the postmodernists usually rejected *a priori* an intervening historical subject, ceding the ground
of metanarrative to the ruling-class.

Capitalism is a system based on the constant destruction and creation of capital. At its most benign this appears as fashion and novelty.
At its more brutal this dynamic appears as shuttered factory gates in
Indiana and bombs falling on Syrian refugees. It appears as six million
dead from COVID-19, as pogroms in India, as Paris police murdering
Algerian youth, as genocide in Palestine. This temporal dialectic — the
unfolding crises born of UCD — is experienced differently depending on one's social class, identity and geographic position. As noted,
the working-class experiences this as a gothic-guturism, or what here is
termed gothic capitalism. What the working-class experiences as barbarism, the bourgeoisie experiences as civilization.

For Laura Hoptman, curator of MoMA's *Forever Now* — as well
as the previously discussed *Beyond Belief* — contemporary painting has
come to exist in a morally neutral miasma of conceptual possibilities:
"Time based terms like progressive — and its opposite, reactionary...
Are of little use to describe contemporary works of art." She continues: "In this new economy of surplus historical references, the makers
take what they wish to make their point or their painting without guilt,
and equally important, without an agenda based on a received meaning of style."[57] In other words, the Gulf War didn't happen in real life,
it only happened on CNN. To be fair, Hoptman accurately describes
how the privileged bourgeois, situated in the center of global cities,
experiences culture as a tourist in space and time. They are disinclined
to respond to the unfolding disasters because they already live in their
own private Elysiums.

The majority of the human race interacts with space and time in a
more constrained manner. They must deal with racist police. They have

---

57 Hoptman, Laura, *The Forever Now: Contemporary Painting in an Atemporal World* (New
York: MoMA, 2015), 15.

to go to work in the morning. They must deal with the Russian or American bombs that threaten their hometowns. They have to pay the rent. They must deal with transphobic politicians and predatory cismen.

STRONG-WEAK IMAGES VS. WEAK IMAGES

It is not the weak image that heralds the apocalyptic erasure of time. Nor does it give voice to those who have been isolated in gothic ruins. The weak image *avoids* the apocalypse around it. It is not the weak image that becomes transcendent. It is the strong image worn by grit that transcends time — for example, from the walls of Chauvet Cave. The cave paintings of Chauvet, in southeast France, date back 35,000 years. On the walls of the cave, there are dozens and dozens of overlapping animals, a human-animal hybrid painted on a stalactite, handprints, and other marks. In Werner Herzog's *Cave of Forgotten Dreams* (2010), the art historians and scientists who study the cave describe an almost mystical relationship with the art and the Paleolithic humans who made it.

Part of this is the auric meaning of ancient cave paintings which we associate with a ritual function. As Benjamin notes of art before the age of technological reproducibility, "the contextual integration of art in tradition found its expression in the cult" — a more or less permanent siting in the church, in temples, buildings of state, and its relations to performances of church and state.[58] "Artistic production begins with ceremonial objects," Benjamin argues. The meaning of the devotional image, handmade books of worship, and icons were bound spatially and conceptually by social ritual, sculpting the *distance* between viewer and image/object. As art patronage shifted from church to the individual bourgeois, and easel painting became a craft industry in every European city and town, cult-value was, according to Benjamin, shifted to "exhibition value."[59] The sculpting of space and distance — in ritual — shapes

---

58 Benjamin, Walter, *The Work of Art in the Age of Its Technological Reproducibility and Other Writings on Media* (Harvard University Press, 2008), 24.
59 Benjamin, *The work of Art in the Age of Its Technological Reproducibility*, 25-27.

the meaning of an artwork. I use the word "distance" because I agree with the art critic Jan Tumlir that Benjaminian aura is about both space and time; and things can be 'distant' in each.[60] Just as a montage or collage changes the meaning of the images placed within it by turning them into a kind of language, the nature and performance of space and distance around an artwork changes its meaning. The reason the paintings at Chauvet speak to us so profoundly is because they are the records of a lost human performance. We read ourselves into the cave. We are seduced into imagining a kind of salvation from our inevitable existential obliteration. Similar things happen when one goes to see Orsen Welles' *Touch of Evil* (1958) in the historic Music Box theater in Chicago. The human ritual of "going to the movies" reshapes the film's meaning.

It is my argument here that the maker of strong-weak images mixes what may be considered weak and strong in an attempt to recover lost meaning — to recast the strong politics and strong images of the past in the context of a weak present.

Artworks as transcendent images connect the precarity of the present to the past and future. They connect our weaknesses to imagined, projected, or historic strengths and traumas. *The transcendent image, therefore, is the image that alternates between weak and strong, like the breathing of a lung.* The future does not belong to poor imitations of Malevich but to men who fly into space from their apartments and women who crawl out of the sea.[61] In Maya Deren's surrealist film, *At Land* (1944), the artist crawls from the ocean onto a beach, and then across a table during a bourgeois dinner party. The guests ignore her. She approaches a man playing chess. When she reaches him, he walks away. A pawn is knocked over. A pattern of displaced or unrecognized subjectivity recurs. She is struggling to overcome some kind of weakness. Ilya Kaba-

---

60 Jan Tumlir was one of my professors at the Sam Fox School of Design and Visual Art. His approach to modernism was largely Hegelian, and he argued, more or less constantly, that aura was a product of both space and time.
61 This is a reference to Ilya Kabakov and Maya Deren.

kov's installation, *The Man Who Flew Into Space from His Apartment* (1989), inverts the symbolic mythology of the USSR towards the dreams of an individual working-class protagonist. The installation, first exhibited in the west in the late 1980s, depicts a small "communal" apartment typical of working-class Muscovites under Stalinism. A seat is attached to a slingshot like device. There is a hole in the ceiling where, presumably, the unseen protagonist flew through the roof of his building. Surrounding the apparatus are images from the USSR space program. As Boris Groys argues:

> [I]n his installation [he] uses images of Red Square and other symbols of the communist, Soviet utopia in order to tell the story of the individual, private fate of the hero of the installation. The great utopian narrative describing how all of humanity would one day be collectively propelled out of the gravitational pull of oppression and misery and into the cosmos of a new, free, weightless life has often enough been dismissed as passé, old-hat, a thing of the past. Yet stories of personal, private dreams and of individual attempts to realize these dreams cannot be told other than with recourse to that good old collective utopian narrative.[62]

The ultimate reason that the story of individual emancipation cannot be told without the "good old collective utopian narrative" is because individual emancipation is only possible through collective liberation. The false socialism of the USSR concealed the truth that democratic socialism from below was the alternative to both western capitalism and eastern "communism." Regardless, Kabakov developed a series of strategies to allow for the suspension of disbelief of modern and pre-modern "utopian dreams." His "total installations" created

---

62 Groys, Boris, and Kabakov, Ilya *The Man Who Flew Into Space From His Apartment* (Afterall, 2006), 21.

a (theatrical) space in which metanarratives could be believed. In the *Palace of Projects* (2000) a structure was constructed that echoed early Soviet Constructivism, including Vladimir Tatlin's famous *Monument to the Third International* (1919-1920). Within that structure were vignettes that communicated "utopian stories" from imaginary citizens of the former Soviet Union. In part this was achieved by creating a fictive space representing "the world" that contained expressive art objects. Kabakov's brilliance was that his installations were *both* weak and strong. They included both "sacred" unique art objects — paintings for example — and mass-produced posters and objects.

The transcendent image belongs to Kazimir Malevich's Cosmist dreams — that brief moment when the idea of individual salvation and collective emancipation seemed to be linked. Cosmism, an esoteric 19th century Russian philosophy, argued that the "common task" of humanity should be the eradication of death and the creation of human immortality. This required the end of war and racism, the colonization of space, and massive spending on the arts. These ideas percolated within the early Soviet avant-garde. The image that is *both weak and strong* connects spiritual and social aspirations to present-day weakness. It acknowledges the contradiction between human potential and its present actuality of immiseration, alienation, oppression, and exploitation. The transcendent image is a column pointing to heaven with its pedestal covered in excrement and bodily fluid. It lives in both the material and spiritual realms of art.

WEAK POLITICAL ART
(OR SITUATIONISM WITHOUT SOVIETS)

The weakness of contemporary art is also found in some of its avowedly political art — such as hopelessly self-referential institutional critiques and the patronizing philanthropy of art as social practice.

A lot of contemporary political art is influenced by Situationism

— the radical French artistic, political and cultural movement associated with the theorist Guy Debord. The Situationists were critical of what they called the "spectacle" of post-war consumer capitalism and proposed two main counterstrategies: dérive and détournement. Dérive referred to unplanned movement through an urban environment, similar to the Benjaminian and Baudelairian idea of the flâneur, as well as the concept of psychogeography. Dérive had the potential, it was thought, to unmake the utilitarianism of the capitalist city and show the urban space for what it truly was (good and bad). In terms of visual art, the concept of détournement held that the dominant images of culture could be remixed and turned on their head. A billboard for Coca-Cola could be altered to expose that company's use of death squads against union organizers in Columbia. The original Situationists had revolutionary working-class politics. They threw themselves into the "French May" — the 1968 student uprising and general strike that nearly toppled the French government — and called for the formation of workers councils or soviets. Many of the present-day political artists inspired by them, however, have jettisoned the revolutionary loyalties of Situationism.

In 1992 cultural theorist Sadie Plant argued for the defanging of Situationism in the following manner:

> The line of imaginative dissent to which Dada, surrealism, the situationists, and the activists of 1968 belong continually reappears in the poststructuralist and desiring philosophies of the 1970s, and the post-modern world view to which they have led is itself faced with the remnants of that tradition..
>
> A cursory reading of poststructuralist thought leaves revolutionary theory without a leg to stand on.
>
> ....although poststructuralism is in some senses a radical break with the situationist project, a host of continuities makes it impossible to oppose the two world views completely. The interests, vocabulary and

style of the situationists reappear in Lyotard's railings
against theory and Foucault's maverick intellectual-
ism... [63]

"Like the situationists," Plant argues, the poststructuralists "observe that the world now seems to be a decentered and aimless collection of images and appearances... and declare the apparent im-
possibility of a future progress and historical foundation."[64] Plant is
wrong here about the Situationists — as noted in their actions in the
French May, they did hold out for progress and historical foundation.
But Plant does describe a number of Situationist inspired currents in
contemporary art, focused on playing with the signs of exploitation
and oppression without any hope of an emancipatory endgame. This
tendency in contemporary political art was crystalized in the discus-
sion surrounding Jennifer Allora and Guillermo Calzadilla's *Track and
Field* assemblage at the Venice Biennale in 2011. An upside-down military tank was installed outside the American pavilion. A treadmill was
placed on the bottom — now top — of the tank. As someone ran on
the tread mill the tank treads would rotate. It seemed to be a criticism
of US militarism in the middle of the ongoing "war on terror." But,
as many people in the art world pointed out, formally and informally,
something about the critique of militarism and power didn't work in
that rarefied context.

Social practice art appears to offer an alternative. Social practice
art tends to be defined as artwork that "involves community" in the
production or construction of an artwork — usually some kind of performance and/or installation. Often, this involves some act of service
from the artist: providing food, for example. However, while there are
exceptions, a great deal of social practice art creates a mechanism for
social interaction without a sense of social criticality. As Claire Bishop

63 Plant, Saide, *The Most Radical Gesture: The Situationist International in a Post-Modern Age*
(Routledge, 1992), 111-112.
64 Plant, *The Most Radical Gesture*, 112.

points out, one of the problems with social practice is this rejection of authorship. An apparently radical gesture becomes highly conservative. Rejecting the author in practice means ratifying the ruling ideas of society (which tend to reject the idea of actual social struggle). "[C]ompassionate identification with the other is typical of the discourse around participatory art," Bishop argues, "in which an ethics of interpersonal interaction comes to prevail over a politics of social justice."[65]

> In insisting on consensual dialogue, sensitivity to difference risks becoming a new kind of repressive norm – one in which artistic strategies of disruption, intervention or over-identification are immediately ruled out as 'unethical' because all forms of authorship are equated with authority and indicted as totalizing.[66]

As the art critic Ben Davis and others note, art gestures focused on distributing food — as has been the case in social practice art organized at the Brooklyn Museum as well as Theaster Gates's *Dorchester Projects* — often work in concert with the neoliberal reduction of the welfare state.[67] I raise this not to criticize individual artists but to point out a convergence of art-as-philanthropy with a decline in social policy. It's as if the art world is supposed to fill the gaps left by declining welfare, only totally insufficiently given its meager resources. On the other hand, the nature of interpersonal service often precludes a radical critique of social ills such as hunger. In the case of the Brooklyn Museum, this fed into existing protests being organized around the "decolonization" of the museum and its overall role in gentrifying the borough. Instead of individual expression or collective liberation, "social practice art" often offers a symbolic philanthropy. The flattening of the social and spiritual

65 Bishop, Claire, *Artificial Hells: Participatory Art and the Politics of Spectatorship* (Verso, 2012), 25.
66 Bishop, *Artificial Hells*, 29.
67 Davis, Ben, "A critique of social practice art," *International Socialist Review* (July 2013).

aspects of art are tied together. The weak images of much social practice art beg Bishop's question. "[T]he aesthetic doesn't need to be sacrificed at the altar of social change," she writes summarizing Jacques Ranciere, "because it always already contains that ameliorative promise."[68]

THE COMMODIFICATION OF THE DEMATERIALIZED

Critic and curator Lucy Lippard's *Six Years: The Dematerialization of the Art Object from 1966 to 1972* sketches how conceptual art was one of art's last great attempts to escape capitalism. Conceptual art emphasized ideas, language and ephemeral performances. It sought to decouple art from object, and in so doing, separate art from commodification. In the decades since 1973 such "utopian" dreams have been torn asunder by daily grinds, the triumph of a worldwide art market and an ongoing suspicion of "grand narratives" — all underpinned by neoliberal capitalism. As Lippard outlines in her essay, "Escape Attempts," the impulse to free art from its institutional fetters and commodity status came with other radical energies of the time: the antiwar, civil rights, Black power, and women's liberation struggles.[69]

The Art Workers Coalition (AWC) was formed in 1969. Minimalist and conceptual art exhibitions were held to benefit the Student Mobilization Committee to End the War in Vietnam. The Ad Hoc Women Artists Committee — connected to AWC — countered the Whitney Museum's lack of female artist representation by issuing a fake press release "stating that there would be fifty present women (and fifty percent non-white)" artists represented in a 1970 sculpture exhibit. The FBI was sent to investigate the fraudulent press release. Interestingly, while many of these artists embraced radical politics for a time, only a few made overtly political works. Most poured their energies into revolutionizing art itself, escaping the confines of the art-object's com-

---

68 Bishop, *Artificial Hells,* 3.
69 Lippard, Lucy, *Six Years: The Dematerialization of the Art Object* (University of California Press, 1997), vi-xxi.

modity status, hoping to make art a free-floating, more democratic, less material process.

A missionary zeal informed the heyday of conceptual art. Lippard recalls:

> [I]n 1969, as we were imagining our heads off … I sus-
> pected that "the art world is probably going to be able
> to absorb conceptual art as another 'movement' and
> not pay too much attention to it. The art establishment
> depends so greatly on objects which can be bought
> and sold that I don't 'expect' it to do much about an
> art that is opposed to the prevailing systems." … By
> 1973, I was writing with some disillusion… "Hopes
> that 'conceptual art' would be able to avoid the gen-
> eral commercialization, the destructively 'progressive'
> approach of modernism were for the most part un-
> founded. It seemed in 1969… that no one, not even a
> public greedy for novelty, would actually pay money, or
> much of it, for a Xerox sheet referring to an event past
> or never directly perceived, a group of photographs
> documenting an ephemeral situation or condition, a
> project for a work never to be completed, words spoke
> but not recorded… Three years later, the major con-
> ceptualists are selling work for substantial sums here
> and in Europe… Clearly, whatever minor revolutions
> in communication have been achieved by the process
> of dematerializing the object… art and artists in capi-
> talist society remain luxuries.[70]

Indeed, conceptualism seemed to turn painters and other artists into gothic anachronisms; beginning a process of memeification that would

---

70 Lippard, *Six Years*, xxi.

later become generalized in digitized finance and social media. When American conceptualism was born, part of its logic flowed from minimalist artists. These artists would produce instructions for the industrial fabricators that actually made the works. This begged the question: is the art the final product or the instructions? This led to more and more experimentation, and a dematerialized art seemingly free from the commodity status of paintings and sculptures. You could make art that was just "instructions" for a performance or an ephemeral artistic gesture. If all you needed was "instructions," a telephone line or mailbox was all that separated an individual from art patronage. Producing an *actual thing* could be seen, for a time, as ratifying the commodity status of an artwork rather than challenging it. In retrospect, however, this can be seen as the early creation of an algorithmic culture. The artwork became a kind of math. Moreover, the instructions — and photographic evidence of ephemeral performances — quickly became commodities themselves.

As Lippard puts it, any escape from art's status as a commodity was only temporary. Art was placed back in its white-walled prison cell. Four things stand out about this in hindsight.

1) From a scientific and strategic standpoint conceptual art's attempt to escape commodity fetishism was doomed from the beginning— as were similar overtures from Fluxus in the early 1960s and Dada in the 1910s and 1920s. Classical Marxism is largely correct that revolution, based on large social forces, is necessary to abolish capitalism and commodity relations, including in the arts.

2) From a theoretical standpoint (in which the point of theory is the actual transformation of systems) conceptualism failed. But without its idealism conceptualism would not have the same meaning. Conceptual art needed to be the product of zealous utopianism. Without the dream the art would not be the same art.

3) The commodification of the dematerialized artwork prefigured the commodification of the (seemingly) dematerialized cultural and communicative space of the Internet. The dematerialization of the

Internet also came into being with a wave of utopianism.

4)   Dematerialization, like automation, promised liberation from com-
     modity alienation and exploitation. Instead, they each delivered a
     devaluing of work.[71]

Ben Davis is right when he argues there is a tendency to give too
much political weight to art. At the same time artists must *believe* their
art has transformative power. The process of creation requires the artist to project a multitude of meanings into her work. The artist must
be, like Jake and Elwood, on a mission from (or against) God. All art
must, quixotically, aim to "change the world" in part or in total. It does
not necessarily matter, from an artistic point of view, that change at the
macro level is impossible. As Marxists we cannot proscribe a political,
conceptual or aesthetic path for art. *As artists*, however, *we must* chart
such paths. This necessity of belief stands in contrast with many of
the dominant ideas of the past few decades that promote a weak art,
steeped in entertainment and irony.

THE DEMOCRATIC IMAGE

The supposedly "strong" images of the dominant culture offer no way
out for the proletarian subject. I refer here to the "dark" realism of
prestige television (*The Sopranos, The Wire*, etc.), the saccharine emotional pornography of Hallmark films, and the endless (sometimes apocalyptic) spectacles of zombie television and superhero films. The weak
images of the academic avant-garde offer little to counter this. The
solution for the class-conscious artist is to connect weakened art and a
weakened working-class to universal aspirations. This strong-weak chi-
mera — whereby weak art is put to the service of class consciousness
— represents an aspirational popular avant-garde. Historically it has
come from outside the art world as often as within it — and sometimes

---

71 See the recent book by Resnikoff, Jason, *Labor's End: How the Promise of Automation
Degraded Work* (University of Illinois Press, 2021).

both, in the work of the Wild-Style graffiti innovators of the 1970s and the punk rock DIY posters and zines of the 1970s and 1980s. Raymond Pettibon, influenced by William Blake and Goya,[72] was part of the early punk visual aesthetic, producing art (including the logo) for his brother's band, Black Flag. The tension between "weak" and "strong" inherent to his work was summarized by Pettibon himself when he argued, "I am really asking ... for you to look at [popular animated figure on postwar US television] Gumby with the same kind of respect that you would if it was some historical figure or Greek statue."[73]

Pettibon's drawings, mostly ink with pen or brush on paper, sometimes presented as "art drawings," comics, and posters, captured US punk antipathies to cultural and political institutions — the church, government, family, etc. — often with sexually suggestive elements. Like comics and punk DIY posters these artworks often employ a great deal of hand-written text. A 1981 drawing, *No Title (Make Me Come)* depicts a policeman with a revolver in his mouth with a word balloon above the gun whose text, presumably "Make Me Come," has been partially erased. A 1984 *Black Flag* record sleeve for *Slip it In* features a nun wrapping her arm around a naked and hairy leg. Pettibon's 1992 drawing, *Gumby*, depicts the titular character literally taking a piss, surrounded by somewhat incoherent handwritten writing, some of which is obscured by other layers of ink or intentionally blurred.

As Benjamin Buchloh observes, Pettibon both continued and argued with the work of Andy Warhol — which had been dismissed by the left and emptied of contradiction and depth by his would-be inheritors.[74] Warhol's *leveling* worked in multiple ways: bringing the popular and "kitsch" into the art space and then reintroducing the mark of

---

72 Enright, Robert, "What Remains To Be Said: An Interview with Raymond Pettibon," *Border Crossings* Vol. 29 Issue 4 (December 2010), 20-35.
73 Buchloh, Benjamin H.D., "Raymond Pettibon: After Laughter," *October* 129 (Summer 2009), 13.
74 Buchloh, "Raymond Pettibon," 15..

the hand (however mitigated through mechanical reproduction) in the flaws of his screen prints. Like Pettibon, Warhol channeled Goya in his own disaster series — *Death in America*.[75] This did not represent popular content per se but *popular concerns*: repressed sexuality and violence (the *Most Wanted Men* series banned at the 1964 World's Fair), and mortality, both individual and social (*Marilyn, Race Riot, 129 Die in Jet*).[76] The *Most Wanted Men* series consisted of large black and white screenprints of the thirteen men "most wanted" by the New York City police department. Originally commissioned for the World's Fair, the fair organizers rejected the work. It is not clear whether they understood the double meaning of the series title, or if they merely objected to the general seediness of the prints. Warhol's queer themes have often been downplayed in popular culture. Similarly, Warhol's disaster prints/paintings were initially far less popular in the US than Europe, as bourgeois Americans seemed unsure how to handle the intersection of glamour and death. *Race Riot* (1964) featured a reproduced news photograph of police dogs attacking civil rights protestors. *129 Die in Jet* (1962) — a painting and print — depicts a recreated black and white newspaper cover announcing the crash of Air France flight 007.

Pettibon and Warhol do not produce weak images but strong-weak images — in the case of Pettibon in the degeneration of the "American Dream" that characterized early punk.[77] His works mirror the actions of the first generation of Wild Style graffiti writers — claiming the urban space as their own, albeit symbolically.[78] Such leveling does not eschew unfolding dystopias (as with the false equality of "atemporal painting" or the milquetoast rebellion of "Hope Punk"[79]) but intro-

---

75 Marcel Krenz, "Art in Times of Disaster," *Art Review* 53 (2002), 26.
76 Krenz, "Art in Times of Disaster," 26.
77 Buchloh, "Raymond Pettibon," 15-16.
78 See Jack Stewart, *Graffiti Kings: New York City Mass Transit Art of the 1970s* (Melcher Media, 2009).
79 Turl, Adam, "Against Hopepunk," *Locust Review* (January 13, 2020): https://www.locustreview.com/blogs/against-hopepunk.

duces social and existential contradictions — free expression vs. the bureaucratic city, disdain for failing official moralities, the death masks of celebrity, images of electric chairs reproduced as fetishes.

As Jamie Reid describes the early punk art milieu:

> The growth of the independent DIY [punk] scene in the late 1970s… resulted in graphic design for record sleeves, posters, flyers, and fanzines that could be targeted to specific, often small-scale, markets. Many of these could be regarded as strongly noncommercial in terms of the mainstream record industry, or in the handmade, labor-intensive nature of the packaging itself. Their designs often involve strategies that, although based on limited budgets, were inventive and sophisticated – incorporating alternative production processes, the adaptation of available, lo-tech materials, and simple, often handcrafted, printing techniques.[80]

Early punk's visual artists recall Arte Povera's use of "poor" materials — in particular the political "igloos" of Mario Merz and the interventions of Michelangelo Pistoletto (*Venus of the Rags* and the *Vietnam* mirror paintings). *Venus of the Rags* (1967) was an assemblage/installation that featured a classical statue of Venus surrounded by piles of ragged clothing. *Vietnam* (1965) depicted an image of an early anti-Vietnam war protest painted on stainless steel, polished into a mirror, placing viewers into the protest itself. Just as punk was born of deindustrialization — and a rolling back of development among industrial workers in the U.S. (and elsewhere) — Arte Povera was born of Italy's post war industrial boom (and antagonism toward U.S. imperialism and art-world arrogance). Arte Povera responded to American-style consumerism with a left-wing cul-

80 Bestley, Russ and Ogg, Alex, *The Art of Punk: The Illustrated History of Punk Rock Design* (Voyageur Press, 2012), 8.

tural romanticism. In 1967 the art critic Germano Celant published "Arte Povera: Notes for a Guerilla War" comparing the group's aesthetic strategies with the national liberation wars raging in Latin America, Africa and Asia.[81] As Nicholas Cullinan writes:

> Celant's characterization of Arte Povera reflects Italy's struggle to reconcile and adapt to its transition from a relatively impoverished and predominantly agrarian country ravaged by World War II to the rapidly industrializing nation propelled by the Marshall Plan-backed miracolo italiano, or economic miracle, in the late 1950s and early '60s. Together with American aid, the growth of companies like the Turin-based automobile company Fiat... contributed to Italy's burgeoning foreign trade. Yet this 'miracle' caused Italy a great deal of social tension and upheaval. A case in point was the dislocation engendered through the geographical and economic schism of mass migration from the poor South to the rich North.[82]

This returns us to the notion of uneven and combined development (UCD) and the way in which capitalism's constant reformation of industry, capital, and labor provokes cultural dislocation. We might ask: What does a weak image — an image that avoids the social and existential crises of the world — mean in deindustrialized St. Louis or Toledo? The reason our images must mix the "strong" and "weak" is because UCD itself surrounds the working-class with weak and strong signs, the "social tension and upheaval" Cullinan cites above. Today, giant digital billboards from the future light up industrial ruins in East

---

81 Cullinan, Nicholas, "From Vietnam to Fiat-nam: The Politics of Arte Povera," *October* 124 (Spring 2008), 8-10.
82 Cullinan, 13, "From Vietnam to Fiat-nam." Of course, Arte Povera operated in the standard commercial idiom of the art market in Italy as well.

Saint Louis. Shakespearean tragedies occur outside a boarded-up KFC in West Virginia. The beauty and *pathos* come from the struggle itself — in the Bronx, in Los Angeles, in the Factory (both Andy's and Fiat's), in Pittsburgh, in Turin.

THE GOTHIC CYBERNETIC

Just as conceptual art prefigured the "dematerialization" of the Internet, the DIY ethos and practice of punk prefigured the early anarchic phase of the Internet. Much as conceptualism was metabolized by the art market, DIY self-publishing, once translated into digital space, was increasingly mediated by capital and the enclosure of large social media platforms by algorithms. This creates something along the lines of what Henri Lefebvre calls "abstract space" in relation to alienated cities.[83] Organic connection and context are removed from interactions. Our images and text appear dematerialized in the social media feed. They are placed into a kind of montage determined by the social media algorithm. With generative AI they are even *created* by the algorithms. By contrast, the way one encountered a zine or self-produced mixtape before the Internet, was facilitated by contradictory spaces with some degree of authenticity, organic connection, and autonomy. These record shops, cafes, dive-bars, and similar places comprise what Lefebvre and David Harvey call "heterotopia" or "spaces of difference."[84] These were neither liberated spaces (directly democratic and post-capitalist) nor spaces overdetermined by capital. They were variable and in flux.

While the Internet — as a mass participatory space — has become ever more contradictory, it has also become wholly shaped in capital's image. Counter-cultural and counter-capitalist memes and gestures are reproduced. But the overall logic is that which Jodi Dean calls "communicative capitalism." Dean argues that the Internet is struc-

---

83 Lefebvre, Henri *The Production of Space* (Blackwell, 1991), 287.
84 See Harvey, David, *Rebel Cities* (Verso, 2019), xvii.

tured by "an ideology of publicity."[85] Noting the insidiousness of this ideology, she writes:

> In effect, changing the system, organizing against and challenging communicative capitalism, seems to require strengthening the very system: how else to get out the message than to raise the money, buy the television time; register the domain names, build the websites, and craft the accessible, user-friendly, spectacular message? Democracy demands publicity.[86]

Written in the early 2000s, at a time of transition, before the algae bloom of the digital image, Dean's argument could seem antiquated. But her core points, and the *contradiction of participation*, remain fundamental: "Precisely those technologies that materialize a promise of full political access and inclusion drive an economic formation whose brutalities render democracy worthless for the majority of people."[87] If there was a moment of relative freedom and anarchic expression in the era of the early Internet, and to some degree there was, this incomplete and problematic digital "commons" was, in effect, *enclosed* by the rise of giant Internet corporations and platforms (Facebook, Google, Twitter, Instagram, Tumblr) as well as legislation.[88] Capitalist ideology is written into the code of the digital space.

The digital codes and algorithms of our cybernetic lives are languages. Most of that code was created by certain human beings at a certain point and time with particular ideas about the world and particular material interests.[89] In this way they reflect ideology in a far more pronounced manner than other tools produced by capitalism. One way

---

85 Dean, Jodi, "Why the Net is not a Public Sphere," *Constellations* Volume 10, No. 1 (Oxford: Blackwell Publishing, 2003), 98.

86 Dean, "Why the Net is not a Public Sphere," 102.

87 Dean, "Why the Net is not a Public Sphere," 98.

88 Dean, "Why the Net is not a Public Sphere," 102-103.

89 Benjamin, Ruha, *Race After Technology* (Cambridge, Mass: Polity Press, 2019).

to think about this is to take Ruha Benjamin's observation of language and code in relation to racism and compare it to an industrial tool such as a lathe. A lathe can be used in a racist way, of course. Black workers can be denied access to its use. Black consumers may not be able to buy products produced by the lathe. But the lathe itself is not racist. Or, more precisely, it does not enact racism that has been built into it. Many programs used to find criminals and automate hiring, however, are racist. Facial recognition software has led to the arrest of innocent Black persons. And hiring software frequently discriminates against people of color.[90] Because computer code is a language it reflects ideology in a far more pronounced manner than many other tools.

The ideologies of Silicon Valley — from its foundation onward — have tended to reflect a certain kind of increasingly right-wing libertarianism. Richard Barbrook and Andy Cameron argued as far back as 1996 (just two years into the "world wide web") in "The Californian Ideology" that the ideological orientation of the Bay Area tech industry was rooted in the separation of Bay Area counterculture from its egalitarian New Left roots. While still messianic and utopian, the ideology of its chief programmers — increasingly flush with capital investment — began to adopt an ideal of "cyborg masters and robot slaves." To maintain this fiction — as their software depended on a great deal of human and cybernetic labor — hardware production was offshored. Cameron and Barbrook compared this to Thomas Jefferson's invention of the dumb waiter, a service lift that could send food from a kitchen up to the main residence — which allowed him to be served dinner by unseen slave labor.[91]

This tendency led to an aggressively middle-class conception of the Internet as a democratic "bazaar" — a petit-bourgeois market, freed of its uncouth laborers — being counterposed to the ideolog-

---

90 Benjamin, *Race After Technology.*
91 Barbrook, Richard and Cameron, Andy, "The Californian Ideology," *Science as Culture,* Vol 6 (1996), 1-15.

ical "cathedral" of higher education, the mass-media, journalism, the State Department, etc.[92] But, because the logic of capital is consolidation-over-time, the bazaar evolved into a weirdly anarchic counter-cathedral, albeit one even more susceptible to paroxysms of hate and conspiracy, and more *directly* influenced by capital. Over time, the right-wing ideology *written* into the script of Silicon Valley code would be expressed in AI generation — the wholesale theft and reconstitution of intellectual work by the "cyborg masters" — and, as David Golumbia notes, the utopian fantasy of a non-state fiat currency in bitcoin and other blockchain "products."[93]

Cyber-utopianism was widespread in the 1990s, often dovetailing in art schools with readings from Foucault, as well as the overall postmodern and post-structuralist ethos of the time. While it is tempting to see this as one-sided (after the enclosure of the Internet), there was a relatively anarchic freedom in the early days of the world wide web (and its predecessors). This was expressed in Donna Harraway's *Cyborg Manifesto* as well as in other queer and feminist documents. Feminists and queer theorists rightly saw the potential of the cybernetic to ease or undo essentialist conceptions of gender and identity; as well as allow for the augmentation of the body.[94] Before the undoing of spaces like MySpace and Tumblr, queer identities could be more freely explored and discussed. Trans and queer youths in small towns could find support and engagement. Moreover, digital communication helped the organization of the Arab Spring, Occupy Wall Street, anti-austerity protests in Greece, and BLM protests in Ferguson, Missouri.

---

92 Raymond, Eric S., *The Cathedral and the Bazaar* (O'Reilly: 1999); Barlow, John Perry, "A Declaration of the Independence of Cyberspace," online paper (1996), distributed widely online in the 1990s, accessed here on March 10, 2022: https://www.eff.org/cyberspace-independence.
93 Golumbia, David, *The Politics of Bitcoin: Software as Right-wing Extremism* (University of Minnesota Press, 2016).
94 Pohl, Rebecca, *An Analysis of Donna Haraway's Cyborg Manifesto* (New York: Routledge/Macat, 2018).

The recent protests in solidarity with Palestine have clearly been shaped by digital communication. Over time, however, the benefits of online communication have often waned (both for the left and for artists).

As Jen Schradie showed in her study of right and left social media use in South Carolina, the structure of the Internet tends to favor the far right.[95] Moreover, the structure of social media — particularly its decontextualization of the discrete image or text into a capitalist idiom and montage — creates *capitalist anti-capitalist* gestures. For example, the "online call-out" — as discussed, albeit imperfectly, by Mark Fisher in "Exiting the Vampire Castle" — *individuates* the confrontation of bigotry and abuse in an almost competitive manner.[96] In an "in real life" (IRL) movement context, it is necessary to combat bigotry and abuse, not just because it is right but in order to maintain and expand the solidarity of the movement. That means the way one confronts bigotry is conditioned by social context. A co-worker in a strike who says something sexist should be argued with. But, unless they persist, they shouldn't necessarily become a pariah. The goal is to win them over. A far-right organizer targeting Planned Parenthood cannot be reasoned with. They *should* become a pariah. Online, often without that contextual knowledge, such "call-outs" can sometimes be unnecessarily destructive.

The online left of the 2010s has been further confused by shifts in the algorithms over the past few years — put in place ostensibly to curb right-wing and "Russian" propaganda and favor the official media

---

95 Schradie, Jen, *The Revolution That Wasn't: How Digital Activism Favors Conservatives* (Harvard University Press, 2019).

96 One of the problematic aspects of Fisher's article, despite Fisher's insights into the problem, is his defense of Russell Brand. At that time, Brand, an empty celebrity husk, appeared to be moving toward radical left politics. Brand, however, was a terrible sexist. In 2023, multiple credible allegations of harassment, assault, and rape were made public against Brand. See Fisher, Mark, "Exiting the Vampire Castle," Open Democracy (November 13, 2013). Available online: https://www.opendemocracy.net/en/opendemocracyuk/exiting-vampire-castle/.

of the old "cathedral." There is a prevailing sense among socialists that their "world has shrunk." Several comrades have asked "where has everyone gone?" They simply no longer see the posts of their comrades on Instagram, Facebook or 'X'. In other words, the US left in the 2010s outsourced much of its communications — its organizational "scaffolding" to borrow from Lenin — to capitalist social media. When capitalism shifted its algorithms it threw parts of that left into isolation. Starting in 2018, and accelerating in 2019 and 2020, major social media platforms were tasked with combating "disinformation." This led to platforms like Facebook boosting the algorithmic reach of legacy media organizations like CNN and *The New York Times* and reducing the algorithmic reach of alternative media (both left and right). At the same time, under pressure to monetize the platforms, posts from "friends" were downplayed in favor of sponsored content (advertisements). Earlier in the 2010s, it was common to discuss the existence of "LeftBook," an informal, national and semi-global network of leftists facilitated by social media. Debates were had by thousands of persons in real time on platforms. These debates were sometimes productive and helped shape left politics. For example, *Red Wedge Magazine* — of which I was a part — successfully helped push back against the "left" anti-immigrant and anti-queer arguments of Angela Nagle who had briefly been championed by *Jacobin*.[97]

From a classical Marxist perspective, the cybernetic represents an increasing fusion (or blurring) of dead labor and living labor — or fixed capital and variable capital. This contradiction can be seen in several ways. On the one hand, dead labor (accumulated capital, the means of production, etc.) may be experienced as a kind of *enslavement* of living labor (the living, breathing, worker). On the other hand, its overgrowth — abundance — is the material basis for a democratic post-capitalist society. This is the classical Marxist understanding of the *relations of produc-*

---

97 See Cummings, Jordy, "I Know Who Else Was Transgressive: Teen Vogue Has Better Politics Than Angela Nagle," *Red Wedge Magazine* (August 2, 2017): http://www.redwedgemagazine.com/online-issue/nagle-review.

tion being in conflict with the *forces of production*. The Internet and cybernetics should ease the transition to an egalitarian society. All information and knowledge can be instantly made available, etc. Every individual can potentially become whatever they wish to be — through cultural, technological, and biological intervention. Instead, cybernetics are artificially policed, shaped by capitalist ideology and the need for capital accumulation, further alienating our "free time" as well as our labor. As the joke goes, AI now writes poetry so you can work at Starbucks.

Borrowing from a more Romantic tradition — as well as the Afrosurrealists and Surrealists — *Locust Review* notes that the cybernetic fusion of living and dead labor is a fusion of the working-class with its ancestors.[98] This can be either a vampiric class relation (as described by Marx) or the beginning of something like the Bolshevik-Cosmist dream of redeeming past generations — the early Soviet avant-garde's incorporation of Cosmist esotericism with social revolution. As noted, Russian Cosmism held that science, art, and space travel should become the "common task" of humanity, thereby enabling the resurrection of all previous generations of human life, and allowing for the immortality of all persons.[99] Bolshevik-Cosmism — as expressed in the science fiction of people like Alexander Bogdanov — proposed a *literal* version of Benjamin's later Marxist-theological argument (an apocatastasis) that the revolutionary generation redeemed all previous generations of the exploited and oppressed. Apokatastasis is the theological concept of the redemption of previous lost souls. Michael Löwy argues that Walter Benjamin incorporates this concept into his understanding of history and class struggle. This was central to his polemic against Social Democratic passivity in his "Theses on History."[100]

---

98 Editorial, "Cyborgs! Shoot the Moon!," *Locust Review* 6 (Autumn 2021), 4.
99 Groys, Boris, ed, *Russian Cosmism* (MIT Press, 2018).
100 Löwy, Michael, *Fire Alarm: Reading Walter Benjamin's 'On the Concept of History,'* (Verso, 2005), 35; Walter Benjamin, "On the Concept of History," (1940), available: https://www.marxists.org/reference/archive/benjamin/1940/history.htm.

A contradiction of the cybernetic is that it *should* free the working-class subject. As argued in the *Locust Review* editorial, "Cyborgs! Shoot the Moon!" — "There are two cybernetics. There is the cybernetics of capital, of alienation and control, a cybernetics of obliterated subjectivity. But there is another cybernetics, embedded as a negation within the other, a cybernetics of solidarity, a cybernetics that can redeem all subjects."[101]

The cybernetic is, in this way, both gothic and futurist, animist and scientific.

A similar contradiction is woven into the dialectic of aura and digital, and into the mechanical reproduction of images/art. The various interpretations of Walter Benjamin's concept of aura — sketched in "The Work of Art in the Age of Its Technological Reproducibility"[102]—tend to fall into two camps. One moves toward an anti-technologic romanticism eschewing Benjamin's communist conclusions, the other toward positivist techno-fetishism that reduces art to mere signification. They are both wrong. The tendency of auric value to wither in the mechanically reproduced image is an *ongoing process* in capitalist culture. The creation, eradication and recuperation of auric value comes from two things primarily: 1) The distance of the image/art fetish (in space and time), and 2) The cultic performance that is imbued in and surrounds that image/art fetish (the *theatrical* organization of that distance). As the "aura-less" mechanically reproduced image ages it tends to recover auric value. Therefore, a photographic reproduction of the *Mona Lisa* may eradicate auric value. But a faded tourist Polaroid of the *Mona Lisa* recovers new auric value. The residue of a human performance coupled with the gothic churn of time embodies it with new "authentic" meaning. There is noth-

See also Bogdanov, Alexander, "Immortality Day," in Groys, Boris, ed. *Russian Cosmism*, 215-228 and Bogdanov, Alexander, *Red Star: The First Bolshevik Utopia* (Indiana University Press, 1984).
101 Editorial, "Cyborgs!," 2.
102 Benjamin, Walter *The Work of Art in the Age of Its Technological Reproducibility*.

ing inherently fascist about aura or anything inherently critical about the reproduced image. Or vice-versa. It is the displacement of our being and consciousness by capitalist time that allows for the fascist manipulation of this dialectic. When we, as communists, respond by "politicizing art" — in Benjamin's phrase — we must understand that we are charged with politicizing *both* the auric and mechanically reproduced image.[103] This can lead to nostalgia for something like a romanticized Eurocentric agrarian utopia on the one hand, and a techno-fascism on the other.

What is true of digital political expression is true of artistic expression. It is also shaped by both capitalist political economy and ideology. In place of social heterotopias, we have an often individualist digital space. As Alexander Billet notes in *Shake the City: Experiments in Space and Time, Music and Crisis*, when we leave our apartments in the morning, going into the alienated city, we are often listening to music on our headphones. We are listening, usually, to a streaming service tailored to us personally and determined by algorithm. The once social aspect of "listening" to music has been desocialized. It is understandable, Billet implies, that we prefer our individual soundtracks to the arrhythmic sounds of the capitalist city. But we have become separate from music's collectivity much as we have become separate from the social collectivity of emancipatory politics.[104]

DIFFERENTIATED TOTALITY, OR THE CARNIVALESQUE

The working-class, a majority of the population defined in relationship to economic production, is the key to the transformation of society. But the working-class is not homogenous. It is defined by its thousands of differences: race, gender, sexuality, nationality, psychologies, cultures, biographies, etc. It cannot come together by subsuming differences. The enemy — neoliberal capitalist culture — depends on the isolation and separation of these elements. A left wing cultural opposition unites

103 Benjamin, Walter *The Work of Art in the Age of Its Technological Reproducibility*, 42.
104 Billet, Alexander, *Shake the City: Experiments in Space and Time, Music and Crisis* (1968 Press, 2022), 1-6, 24.

these in a *differentiated totality*. It comes together without sacrificing the subjectivities of its constituent parts. It avoids vulgar Marxism as well as the fatalism of postmodernism. It echoes Mikhail Bakhtin's ideas of the carnivalesque, taken from Rabelais, fused with the avenging crowds of a Zola novel.

Rabelais borrowed his ideas of the carnivalesque directly from the peasants of late medieval France, collecting wisdom "from the popular elemental forces" of "idioms, sayings, proverbs, school farces, from the mouth of fools and clowns."[105] Key to the presentation of a chaotic totality — *a threatening diversity* — in Rabelais is the carnival. The medieval carnival institutionalized a reversal of fortune — the weak would be strong (or the strong would be ridiculed), the powerful would serve — in events such as "the feast of fools" or the "feast of the ass." Orchestrated spectacles aimed to, albeit in a confused manner, democratize the medieval commons through:

1. *Ritual spectacles:* carnival pageants, comic shows of the marketplace.
2. *Comic verbal compositions:* parodies both oral and written, in Latin and the vernacular.
3. *Various genres of billingsgate:* curses, oaths, popular blazons.[106]

"In the framework of class and feudal political structure this specific character could be realized without distortion only in the carnival and in similar marketplace festivals," Michael Holquist writes, "they were the second life of the people, who for a time entered the utopian realm of community, freedom, equality, and abundance."[107]

This "temporary liberation" from the "established order" was pro-

---

105 Michelet, cited in the introduction, Holquist, Michael, to Bakhtin, Mikhail, *Rabelais and His World* (Indiana University Press, 1984), 2.
106 Holquist, Bakhtin, *Rabelais and His World*, 5, 7.
107 Holquist, Bakhtin, *Rabelais and His World*, 9.

gressively abolished with the rise of capitalism and the industrial revolution — but democratic aspirations found new paths.[108] Gustave Courbet's
A Burial at Ornans famously translated his anarchist politics[109] into the
Salon of 1850-1851.[110] Compared to academic painters, Courbet's painting was described as having an "anti-composition" – in that no figure is
given primacy over any other.[111] "Courbet's democracy of vision," Linda
Nochlin writes, "his additive, egalitarian composition, were seen as the
concomitants of a democratic social outlook."[112] The painting depicts a
crowd at a funeral — possibly a metaphorical funeral for the defeat of
the 1848 revolution (famously discussed by Marx in the *18ᵗʰ Brumaire*).
Produced as a series of separate portraits of his fellow citizens, Courbet
makes his hometown equal in the face of death.[113] A similar aesthetic
would permeate much of 20th century muralism — particularly as seen
in the murals of its greatest practitioners, the Mexican muralists, who
were highly influenced by radical (Marxist) politics. Courbet and Diego
Rivera alike foreshadowed the "all-over" uniform aesthetic championed
by Clement Greenberg in New York School abstraction, whereby all por-
tions of an abstract canvas had equal coverage and importance.[114]

Of course, there is a weakness to much modern "democratic"
presentation in that it often lacks the bodily chaos of the medieval
carnivalesque, and therefore the full diverse and anarchic quality of the
working-class. Keith Tyson's installation, *Large Field Array* (2007) is of-

---

108 Holquist, Bakhtin, *Rabelais and His World* 11.

109 Antliff, Alan *Anarchy and Art: From the Paris Commune to the Fall of the Berlin Wall*
(Vancouver: Arsenal Pulp Press, 2007), 17-36. Courbet, a follower of Proudhon,
played a role in the Paris Commune of 1871, leading the destruction of the Vendome
Column, a symbol of French militarism. Courbet was imprisoned and later renounced
his actions during the Commune, therefore escaping execution.

110 Nochlin, Linda, *Courbet* (Thames and Hudson: 2007), 19.

111 Nochlin, *Courbet,* 20.

112 Nochlin, *Courbet,* 24.

113 Nochlin, *Courbet ,* 27.

114 See Kleeblatt, Norman L., et al, *Action/Abstraction* (Yale Press and the Jewish
Museum, 2009).

ten pointed to as an example of rhizomatic work. Many of the discrete objects and images placed into the overall installation are quite interesting and beautiful. But they are dispersed on the floor and walls in an almost perfect grid. The meanings of the individual objects are meant to reshape the meanings of the other objects and the whole. Their bodily separation, however, recreates the overall logic of the white cube gallery space. This tends to contradict, it would seem, the original conception of the 'rhizomatic'.

Gilles Deleuze and Félix Guattari's concept of the rhizome is eclectic and is often described as post-structuralist — a sort of "non-linear" network or pattern.[115] Rhizome refers to the interrelated root system of trees or flora. It is seemingly nonhierarchical. The popularity of this idea made sense during the neoliberal turn, the rise of postmodernism, globalization, and networked computers. It describes real patterns of being and aspects of production — and their cultural expressions — but misses the materiality beneath the patterns (and the ongoing hierarchies of that materiality) as well as the shaping of those patterns by capital.

The concept has been important in more dynamic works of art. See, for example, the paintings of Julie Mehretu and the installation work of Sarah Sze. Deleuze and Guattari present the rhizome as a kind of end of history (although they also present it going back and forth in time). Events become nodes rather than historic developments. This bears similarity to the conception of power in Foucault, and a rejection of vulgar Marxist and Hegelian teleologies. But it is largely a *descriptive* theory. Things flow but the determination of their flow becomes an unknown.[116]

Marxist art, however, cannot merely respond with a new "epic" of combining archetypes. It must aim toward fusing a massively varied constellation of individual subjectivities and cultural identities – united

115 Adkins, Brent, *Deleuze and Guattari's A Thousand Plateaus: A Critical Introduction and Guide* (Edinburgh University Press, 2015).
116 Adkins, *Deleuze and Guattari's A Thousand Plateaus*.

objectively (if not yet subjectively) against forces that oppress and exploit them.[117]

THE ART OF PRIMITIVE COMMUNISM

One of the problems of the weak avant-garde is in its tendency to reject the spiritual and social origins of art itself. This dynamic can be found both among would-be "art entrepreneurs" and progressive artists (who wrongly believe their role is to demystify art). Both, in the end, risk becoming the Thomas Gradgrinds of contemporary art. Thomas Gradgrind is the school superintendent in Charles Dickens' novel *Hard Times* who has a thoroughly utilitarian and mercantile attitude. For example, he mocks a young girl for loving horses without knowing a great deal about them practically. Gradgrind embodies the calculated self-interest and cruelty of the English industrial revolution. The Thomas Gradgrinds of art likewise reduce artistic expression to a kind of utilitarianism. On the "right" this is often expressed in financial terms. On the "left" it can be expressed as a vulgar didacticism.

The Austrian art critic Ernst Fischer, building on Friedrich Engels' "The Role of Labor in the Transition from Ape to Man," discusses art's pre-history in his 1959 book, *The Necessity of Art.* "The Role of Labor" along with *The Origin of Family. Private Property, and the State* (1884) provide the original Marxist exposition of "primitive communism." Engels argues, based on then available anthropological evidence, that hunter-gatherer societies, for the most part, lived in relatively egalitarian relationships without the coercion of a "state," with shared production and access to consumption of goods. This "idyllic" but precarious state-of-being lasted until the mastery of agriculture. Agriculture allowed for the creation of an economic surplus. This surplus enabled the eventual division of society into social classes. While *The Origin of the Family* discusses the

---

117 Of course doing this fully is impossible — it is the political art equivalent of the sublime.

transition from primitive communism to class society, "The Role of La-bor" discusses the transition from a state of nature to conscious hunt-er-gatherer societies — to primitive communism.

The mastery of tools produced social knowledge — the abstrac-tion and generalization of the world. This created a wealth of practical knowledge, but it also created a method of knowing that far surpassed what could be known. "With the use of tools," Fischer argues, "nothing is, in principle, any longer impossible."[118] Words themselves became "magic." Early humans named the seasons, aspects of sexual repro-duction, named the flora and fauna. This gave our ancestors a feeling of immense power. Naming things that could not be fully understood (death, life, love, etc.) would logically extend that power. "[I]n creating art," prehistoric man (sic), "found himself a real way of increasing his power and enriching his life. The frenzied tribal dances before a hunt really did make the warrior more resolute and were apt to terrify the enemy. Cave paintings of animals really helped to build the hunter's sense of security and superiority over his prey."[119] Fischer's overall the-sis is correct, although his thinking is limited by his time. The "magic rite" explanation has been discredited — although it was a commonly held theory in the 1950s.[120] One blow to this theory is the evidence that women produced at least half of prehistoric cave painting. Because it was assumed, again problematically, that there was a gendered divi-sion of labor in these societies between hunters (male) and gatherers (female), it would seem unlikely that "hunting" would be the primary concern of women painters. The main problem, however, is archeolog-ical evidence that shows that the animals depicted in cave and rock art are often not the animals these hunter-gatherers hunted or consumed.

Various ideas have replaced the "magic rite" explanation for cave

---

118 Fischer, Ernst, *The Necessity of Art* (Verso, 2010) 28.
119 Fischer, *The Necessity of Art*, 28-31, 47.
120 see Whitley, David, *Cave Paintings and the Human Spirit* (Prometheus, 2008) and Lewis-Williams, David, *The Mind in the Cave* (Thames and Hudson, 2002).

art. Possessed by a poststructuralist fear of generalization, some of these theories over-emphasize the data of a particular location — the San Rock Art of South Africa or Chauvet Cave in France for example — and refuse to draw wider conclusions (even when the data demands such generalization). A debate ensued between the so-called "pluralists" on the one side and the "shamanistic" model on the other.[121] Essentially, the "pluralist" anthropological approach is associated with post-structuralism. Post-structuralism is a contradictory set of ideas. However, it has tended to eschew "authoritative voices" in favor of a focus on particulars and differences. In terms of approaching prehistoric art and culture, this means rejecting the Marxist idea of primitive communism, as well as other attempts to generalize about hunter-gatherer societies. In contrast, other researchers, sometimes influenced by Marxist ideas, have tried to generalize from anthropological evidence. The best researchers, on both sides, rightly reject the crude gender and racial assumptions made by earlier anthropologists.

CAVE PAINTING AND SHAMANISM

David Lewis-Williams and Thomas Dowson were among the first to argue that much cave painting and rock art was shamanistic[122] — based on studies of San Rock Art and the analysis of phosphenes and abstract motifs.[123] Phosphenes are light patterns not caused by external input — usually the product of hallucinations caused by hunger (fasting), movement (whirling dervishes or dance), intoxication or sleep deprivation. They evidence a central feature of shamanism — entering altered states of consciousness to visit the "spirit world." Of shamanism Lewis-Williams states:

---

121 see Whitley, *Cave Paintings and the Human Spirit*, Lewis-Williams, David and Hodgson, Derek, "Shamanism, Phosphenes and Early Art: An Alternative Synthesis," *Current Anthropology* Volume 1, Number 5 (December 2000).
122 Lewis-Williams and Hodgson, "Shamanism, Phosphenes and Early Art," 866.
123 Lewis-Williams and Hodgson, "Shamanism, Phosphenes and Early Art," 866.

Today this is a disputed word. Some researchers feel that the term has been used too generally to be of any use… I, and many others disagree. We believe that "shamanism" usefully points to a human universal – the need to make sense of shifting consciousness – and the way in which this is accomplished especially, but not always, among hunter-gatherers.[124]

Jean Clottes, former director of research at Chauvet Cave, agrees with Lewis-Williams. "Clottes and Lewis-Williams," David Whitley writes, "argued, in essence, that the caves themselves were topographic models of the trance experience. As the 'entrails of the underworld,' they were the vortex that, through ritual trance, the shaman used to access the supernatural."[125] It was a common practice, in fact, for apprentice shamans to pretend to die before becoming full shamans. Before they could serve their social functions, they had to be "born again" as subjective individuals.

THE ANTI-SHAMANS

The poststructuralists or pluralists counter that this interpretation ignores the specific cultural experiences that produced each artifact. But as Whitley argues:

That the art is in caves as different as Chauvet and Lascaux could reasonably be interpreted as shamanistic in origin… is no small conclusion. As Jean Clottes has repeatedly pointed out, this speaks to the fact that Paleolithic art reflects an extremely long cultural, artistic, and religious tradition – one that lasted for more than twenty thousand years.[126]

---

124 Lewis-Williams, *The Mind in the Cave*, 132.
125 Whitley, *Cave Paintings and the Human Spirit*, 47.
126 Whitely, *Cave Paintings and the Human Spirit*, 76.

Whitley, however, is wrong when he asserts that shamanistic cave painting and rock art reflected an "inner" vs. "outer" practice.[127] Shamanistic art reflected both the immediate social and material needs of a group as well as its spiritual and existential practices. The prehistoric shaman was a priest, healer, joker, historian, storyteller, magician and scientist. Any quest to the spirit world was taken in a dialectical relationship with the needs, material and spiritual, of the hunter-gatherer group.[128] Derek Hodgson argues that Lewis-Williams' shamanistic theory requires a "substantial leap of faith."[129] But the fact that cave painting does not limit itself to the marks associated with phosphenes and that such paintings are also "processed by different regions of the visual cortex"[130] does not negate the shamanistic interpretation thesis. The modern and bourgeois impulse toward categorization and specialization did not exist in egalitarian hunter-gatherer societies. Shamanistic art mixed the complex social, existential and cultural dynamics of early humans. Lewis-Williams answers this charge by looking at the interplay of mythology and ritual in San Rock Art,[131] arguing that posing the question as either/or (myth vs. ritual) misses the point. The San are an indigenous southern African group that persisted as hunter-gatherers well into the 20th century. They were forced to adapt to agriculture during various modernization campaigns in the 1940s and 1950s. Nevertheless, this means their traditional artistic practices — including rock art — persisted longer than in many other societies.[132]

> Metaphors of trance permeate many myths... Certain components of trance experience derive from

---

127 Whitley, *Cave Paintings and the Human Spirit* , 77.
128 See Joseph Campbell, *The Masks of God Volume 1: Primitive Mythology* (Penguin, 1991).
129 Lewis-Williams and Hodgson, "Shamanism, Phosphenes and Early Art," 870.
130 Lewis-Williams and Hodgson, "Shamanism, Phosphenes and Early Art," 869.
131 Lewis-Williams, *The Mind in the Cave*, 105.
132 Lewis-Williams, *The Mind in the Cave*, 105.

the functioning of the human nervous system. For example, sensations of floating or flying in a realm above (sometimes suggested by feathers or wings) and penetrating the ground below via some sort of tunnel (or through water) are hard-wired human neurological experiences... They structure not only many San myths but mythology worldwide; all religions have an ecstatic component, though extreme altered states of consciousness are not necessarily experienced by all adherents.[133]

Both a social-narrative and a subjective experience permeate the art. There is no categorical separation between the existential individual and the collective mythology. They both exist at one and the same time.

There is... no evidence that an independently generated mythology determined trance experience. What the San talk about after trance experiences... and what is painted in the rock shelters both concern the same spiritual realm, the one in which many myths take place... The San painted neither generalized 'mythology' nor specific narratives, but rather their own forays into the spirit realm.[134]

This means, already in the earliest human societies, art was concerned equally with the mundane and fantastic, the group and the individual. In other words, we were already making images that were both "weak" and "strong." This work is "weak" in that it reflects the actuality of material precariousness. It is "strong" in that it imagines entire mythologies and worlds.

133 Lewis-Williams, J.D., "Rock Art: Myth and Ritual, Theories and Facts," *The South African Archeological Bulletin* Volume 61, No. 183 (June 2006) 107.
134 Lewis-Williams, J.D., "Rock Art: Myth and Ritual," 108.

THE IDOLATRY OF SHADOWS

Of course, there are fundamental differences between contemporary art and the art of primitive communism — but art continues to hold a dual social-spiritual functionality expressed in both individual subjectivity and group mythology. Among the anthropologists it is those arguing for the shamanistic interpretation that are following a dialectical materialist approach to their subject — using empirical data toward probable generalizations of social and cultural movements. The post-structuralists, with their devotion to specificity, are trapped by their philosophical idealism.

3. THE ART SPACE AS EPIC THEATER[135]

Ilya Kabakov: Total Installation—Emory Douglas: Expressionist Agit-Prop—William Kentridge: Double Performances—Auric Crisis and the Digital Gesamtkunstwerk—The Organization of Cultic Performance—Social Practice Art—Relational Aesthetics as Crisis—We Are All Outsiders Now—Lessons from Outside—Immortality of Things

Contemporary artists struggle with ongoing structural inequities (a totalizing problem), what has been called "zombie formalism" (an echo of the essentializing modernist art gesture without that gesture's historic avant-garde role) and a weak political art. Zombie formalism was a phrase coined, it seems, by Walter Robinson in a 2014 article on *ArtSpace*. Robinson writes:

> One thing I'm hearing these days, loud and clear, is the hum of an art style that I like to call Zombie Formalism. "Formalism" because this art involves a straightforward, reductive, essentialist method of making a painting (yes, I admit it, I'm hung up on painting), and "Zombie" because it brings back to life the discarded aesthetics of Clement Greenberg, the man who championed Jackson Pollock, Morris Louis, and Frank Stella's "black paintings," among other things.[136]

This work, however, failed to match the substance of Jackson Pollock's paintings or those of other abstract expressionists who

---

135 This chapter incorporates material from the author's written MFA thesis, "Toward an Evicted Art," papers presented at Historical Materialism conferences, and articles in *Red Wedge Magazine*, *Imago*, and *Locust Review* in the 2010s and 2020s.
136 Robinson, Walter, "Flipping and the rise of Zombie formalism," *ArtSpace* (April 3, 2014): https://artspace.com/magazine/contributors/see_here/the_rise_of_zombie_formalism-52184.

sought to cultivate a unique subjective expression to counter the consumer culture and post-war anti-Communist conformity that took hold
in the United States.

Regardless, structural and ideological problems have tended to narrow the art object, space and gesture. Danica Radoschevich argues:

> Though exhibition practices have been scrutinized for
> decades, the formalist "white cube" remains an inter-
> national gallery standard for the exhibition of modern
> and contemporary artwork. Simon Sheikh ... identifies
> that "gallery spaces and museums are still white cubes,
> and their ideology remains one of commodity fetish-
> ism and eternal value... The sustained predominance
> of the white-cube is especially fraught with respect to
> the art market in post bailout New York, wherein a re-
> cession era boom speaks powerfully to the character of
> American late-capitalism. This circumstance indicates
> the artist's subservience to the inordinately wealthy, and
> complicity in their gratuitous consumer desires in an
> era of severe and increasing economic stratification...
> A number of artists and critics deride modern formal-
> ism because it has historically privileged artists, whose
> work is not framed with respect to identity, thereby triv-
> ializing the works of artists who are canonically and/
> or socially marginalized. But even these artists' works
> are almost always exhibited in the inert, white walled
> formalist gallery... This pernicious double bind speaks
> to the paradoxes of the supremacy of formalist values
> in the contemporary art world.[137]

This raises the need for an alternative idea of the art object, gesture and space — one that reasserts the idea of narrative (*a proletarian*

---

137 Radoshovich, "Zombie Gallery."

subject), metanarrative (*the idea of totalizing systemic change*) and recasts the art space as theater (*as an ancient spiritual and social platform*). This is in direct opposition, for example, to the false atemporality expressed in Laura Hoptman's *Forever Now* exhibition. A theatrical art-model poses a radical *temporality* and therefore reasserts the political and existential. As Alain Badiou writes:

> ...Politics takes place, from time to time. It begins, it ends. And, similarly, from the fact that a theater production requires the simultaneous and ordered presence of the seven elements, it follows (and this is an essential triviality) that a theatrical spectacle begins and ends. Representation takes place. It is a circumscribed event. There can be no permanent theatre.
>
> ...everything in it, or almost everything, is mortal.[138]

The art space is a stage, and as Badiou argues, the stage summons the crowd. Therefore, it is inherently political as it mimics but is not identical to the state.[139] The seven elements, noted above, according to Badiou, are "place, text, director, actors, décor, costumes and public."[140] While there are clear parallels to the art space the comparison is not perfect — nor does it need to be. The art space is somewhat more "irrational" than the theatrical space. It is more irrational because it lacks the theater's clear narrative structure and norms. The "perishable" nature of both, however, is key. Of particular importance are artists who deal with a kind of narrative conceptualism, focused on subjects whose concerns exist in significant part outside the realm of art, constrained by their position within larger systems. The centrality of narrative gives new life to the concepts of Brechtian theater within contemporary art. Brecht sought to engage the audience, appealing to

---

138 Badiou, Alain, *Rhapsody for the Theatre* (Verso, 2013), 11.
139 Badiou, *Rhapsody for the Theatre*, 2-6.
140 Badiou, *Rhapsody for the Theatre* , 11.

the traditional emotional and visual snares of the dramatic arts, while alternatively "distancing" the audience from those tropes. The goal was to spur a proletarian audience into action — towards social revolution. Brecht would use the traditional methods of theater — songs, lighting, drama and melodrama. But he would also expose them — breaking the fourth-wall, leaving the stage curtain partially drawn, placing the musicians on the stage itself, and sometimes even walking on stage in the middle of a play to read *The Communist Manifesto* (often to the frustration of collaborators such as the avant-garde composer Kurt Weill). This undermined the tropes of "culinary theater" (theater meant for entertainment more than enlightenment). In *The Threepenny Opera* Brecht and Weill mocked "high opera" with Weill's appropriation of popular music. But the exposure of these tropes also required the use of these tropes. Brechtian theater moved back and forth between the social and the spiritual, like the breathing of a lung, creating both belief and disbelief, rapture and criticality.

Today, it is *disbelief* that reigns supreme in the art world, an echo of postmodern cynicism and the ongoing conditioning of capitalist realism. To *interrupt this disbelief,* we need to employ a similar alternation between distancing and distance eliminating tropes. *An electric shock can both stop and start a human heart.*

In Ilya and Emelia Kabakov's installation, *The Man Who Flew Into Space From His Apartment* (1989), the protagonist is an archetypal resident of the collective apartments in which working-class Muscovites were once forced to live. A small room is surrounded by images of the Soviet space race. In its center there is a Coyote-Road-Runner like slingshot device. In the ceiling there is a hole, where presumably the man in question escaped his mundane Soviet housing. In *Felix in Exile* (1994), an animated film of charcoal drawings, South African artist William Kentridge presents his alter ego, exiled from the apartheid state, confronted by what he has left behind, including the surveillance of state barbarism. This surveillance prefigures the coming revelations of

South Africa's Truth and Reconciliation Commission. A Black woman looks through surveyor's equipment at the evidence of apartheid's crimes.

These works use distancing techniques, but they also communicate the necessity of a theatrical belief.

ILYA KABAKOV: TOTAL INSTALLATION

It is necessary to acknowledge Ilya Kabakov's "Total Installation." Kabakov's origins were in the underground Moscow conceptual movement. As such his first international works tended to invert the symbolic mythology of the USSR towards the dreams of *individual* working-class and archetypal figures of Soviet life. As Boris Groys describes *The Man Who Flew Into Space from His Apartment*:

> [I]n his installation he uses images of Red Square and other symbols of the communist, Soviet utopia in order to tell the story of the individual, private fate of the hero of the installation. The great utopian narrative describing how all of humanity would one day be collectively propelled out of the gravitational pull of oppression and misery and into the cosmos of a new, free, weightless life has often enough been dismissed as passé, old-hat, a thing of the past. Yet stories of personal, private dreams and of individual attempts to realize these dreams cannot be told other than with recourse to that good old collective utopian narrative.[141]

Of course, the ultimate reason that the story of individual emancipation cannot be told without the "good old collective utopian narrative" is because individual emancipation is only possible through collective liberation. The false socialism of the USSR concealed the truth that democratic socialism from below was the alternative to both western

---

141 Groys, Kabakov, *The Man Who Flew Into Space From His Apartment*, 21.

capitalism and eastern "communism." Regardless, Kabakov developed a series of strategies *to allow for the suspension of disbelief of modern and pre-modern "utopian dreams."* In part this was achieved by creating a fictive space representing "the world" that *contained within it expressive art objects*. For Kabakov this has often been Cezannist paintings. Cezannism was a painting style which mimicked the work of Cezanne and was popular among a small layer of dissident artists before the rise of Moscow Conceptualism.

EMORY DOUGLAS: EXPRESSIONIST AGIT-PROP

In the mid-1960s African American artist Emory Douglas made props for the Black Communications Project in the Bay Area—a theater collective that included the poet Amiri Baraka. Douglas produced theatrical flats — background paintings that are easily moved and changed between acts or plays — developing what Baraka would describe as an "expressionist agit-prop."[142] In 1967 Douglas joined the nascent Black Panther Party for Self Defense (BPP), eventually becoming its Minister of Culture, and devoting his artistic skills, for the next decade, to the party. Douglas would design or supervise much of the art in the *Black Panther* (the BPP's newspaper) and would introduce a weekly poster to be printed along with the newspaper. These images tended to fuse hand-made drawings, often featuring heavy black lines reminiscent of some African designs, caricatures that recalled George Grosz, along with Constructivist and John Heartfield-like photo-collages. This combination of mechanically reproduced images with subjective hand-made expressionism mimicked the distancing techniques of Epic Theater. The stories Douglas told were the heroic BPP battles with racism, war, capitalism and the police, as well as the stories of "regular" African Americans' everyday lives. There was both

142 Durant, Sam, *Black Panther: The Revolutionary Art of Emory Douglas* (Rizzoli, 2007), 176.

collective struggle and subjective personality — whether it was that of Douglas, a single mother, or grotesque subjectivity of the "pigs." Douglas did not merely aim to make propaganda (although he did so brilliantly). He (along with the BPP) aimed to construct a counter-mythology, to "fuse everyday Black life with a revolutionary spirit."[143]

> As Laura Mulvey argues in her essay, "Myth, Narrative, and Historical Experience," "moving from oppression and its mythologies to a stance of self-definition is a difficult process and requires people with social grievances to construct a long chain of counter myths and symbols."[144]

With the passage of time, the older work of Douglas has taken on an ephemeral and gothic character. The newspapers and posters have become, in part, indexical records of the political performance of the BPP, a second layer of auric distancing. The recuperation of Douglas by the art world has given him the chance to preserve the memory of the BPP in a new arena, and his past work has often been presented (rightly) in a theatrical manner. The inclusion of Douglas in the art space is an opportunity — not just for Douglas (although this recognition is well deserved) — but an opportunity to change the nature of the art space itself.

WILLIAM KENTRIDGE: DOUBLE PERFORMANCES

South African artist William Kentridge also got his start in agit-prop theater. Kentridge, however, became ambivalent about the project and its ability to communicate the depth of the alienation and suffering he witnessed:

---

143 Durant, *Black Panther*, 105, 97, 101.
144 Colette Gaiter in Durant, *Black Panther*, 97-98.

We would stage a play which showed domestic workers how badly they were being treated, implying that
they should strike for equal rights. This would be presented in a hall with four thousand domestic workers...There was a false assumption about the public, in
that we 'knew' what 'the people' needed, so I stopped
my involvement with these groups. The early twenti-
eth-century German Expressionists, such as Otto Dix
and Max Beckmann, as well as the early Soviet filmmakers and designers of propaganda posters, had a
way of using their anger, drawing it quite directly, that
corresponded to what I was feeling at the time.[145]

Kentridge's art was shaped by his position as a witness to apartheid — the white Jewish child of anti-apartheid attorneys. Kentridge
could escape the direct barbarity inflicted on Black South Africans. His
work became shaped by his experience with theater (on the one hand)
and inter-war European expressionism and propaganda on the other
— allowing him to assert a human subjectivity in an inhuman contex-
t:[146] Adorno's much-quoted proclamation about the end of lyric poetry (the famed and often mis-contextualized "there can be no poetry"
following the Holocaust) was directly followed by his assertion that
literature must resist this verdict."[147]

In 1979, after years of struggling with painting, Kentridge produced a series of monoprints, fusing drawing and the theatrical. The
series, *Pit*, created a small mise-en-scene — a kind of theatrical series
of persons trapped in a dank pit.[148] Sometime later Kentridge began his
"signature" works of charcoal drawings turned into film animations;

145 Cameron, Dan, Christov-Bakargiev, Carolyn and Coetzee, J.M., *William Kentridge*
(Phaidon, 2010, 15.
146 Cameron, Christov-Bakargiev, Coetzee, *William Kentridge*, 10.
147 Cameron, Christov-Bakargiev, Coetzee, *William Kentridge*, 13.
148 Cameron, Christov-Bakargiev, Coetzee, *William Kentridge*, 16-17.

animations in which you can see the residual marks of previous itera-
tions of drawing. These works were based around a series of fictional
characters: Soho Eckstein (a white, presumably Jewish, South African
businessman), Felix Teitlebaum (a white, presumably Jewish, South African artist) and Mrs. Eckstein (Soho's wife and Felix's lover). Around
these characters the struggles of South African apartheid and the early
1990s transition unfold. The residual marks of the drawing serve as a
Brechtian device for Kentridge:

> The principle is that there's a double performance:
> you watch the actor and the puppet together. The
> process recalls Brechtian theatre: the actors focus on
> the puppets and the audience has a circular trajecto-
> ry of vision from the puppets to the actors and back
> to itself. It's about the unwilling suspension of disbe-
> lief. In spite of knowing that the puppet is a piece of
> wood operated by an actor, you find yourself ascrib-
> ing agency to it.[149]

Felix in Exile (1994) captures Felix Teitlebaum, Kentridge's "sensi-
tive" alter-ego, in exile from South Africa on the eve of its first General Election. In a small hotel room Felix is surrounded by drawings and
images of a Black African woman, Nandi, who surveys the violence
of the Apartheid state (prefiguring the Truth and Reconciliation commission). Echoing previous films in the series, such as *Mine* (1991) (in
which strikers miners confront the gluttony of Soho Eckstein, among
other things), *Felix in Exile* portrays a resigned complicity in which
white South Africans witness the unraveling of the apartheid regime—
resigned, in part, because of the compromise that allowed the economic order to survive the political transition.[150]

---

149 Cameron, Christov-Bakargiev, Coetzee, *William Kentridge*, 19.
150 Cameron, Christov-Bakargiev, Coetzee, *William Kentridge*, 45.

AURIC CRISIS AND THE DIGITAL GESAMTKUNSTWERK

The questions of installation art — and related questions of social practice art and relational aesthetics — are mostly important in light of a crisis of art and its social positioning. What is the unique art image, object or gesture's *function, purpose, and existential raison d'etre* in a world of viral imagery that seems to constantly self-reproduce everywhere? Claire Bishop notes a "difficulty in meaning"[151] in installation art. What exactly is it? At a practical level, she provides two definitions: "1. An arrangement of the artworks in an exhibition. 2. A kind of art in which the space and the ensemble of elements within it are integral elements of the whole artwork."[152]

To tease this out, all art installation is the *construction and sculpting of a cult performance* that surrounds art objects, images, narratives, or gestures, as a singular or collective artwork.[153] The cultic performance is what creates or elaborates *auric* value and meaning. While Benjamin initially referred to religious performance — processionals and liturgies — that surrounded altarpieces and icons, I am extending the meaning to other social performances that surround a work. The social performances surrounding a painting in a salon or art gallery or the social performances that surround a mural running along the train tracks in Chicago's Pislen neighborhood. These social performances, like cultic performances of the church, create auric value. This auric value constitutes an IRL montage where contextualization and human performances shift the *meaning* of the artwork. For example, as Ben Davis notes, it was in no small part the touring of Picasso's *Guernica* to raise money for the Spanish Republic that shaped the meaning of the painting as anti-war and anti-fascist

---

151 Bishop, Claire, *Installation Art* (Tate Publishing, 2005), 5.
152 Bishop, Claire and Arguello, Gemma "Towards a Philosophy of Installation Art," *Journal of Aesthetics and Art Criticism* 78 (3), (June 2020), 333-338.
153 "Cult performance" here refers to Watler Benjamin's conception of cult-performance of the situated art object: see further on in this essay.

imagery.[154] The painting itself contains a number of surreal images of suffering. But there is nothing concrete in the image that makes it clear that it references the Spanish Civil War other than its title — named after a town bombed by Nazi Germany. That meaning is projected by the human performances that surround the painting. Similarly, the meaning of the original Diego Rivera mural, *Man at the Crossroads*, is inter-related to its destruction at Rockefeller Center. That fresco, depicting a worker at the center operating a machine, is surrounded by images of science and disease, of wealth and privation, of fascism and class struggle. The image takes on a tragic performance because of its destruction at the hands of the American capitalist who commissioned it. Nelson Rockefeller ordered the destruction of the painting in 1933, angry that the painting, still in progress, included an image of the Russian Revolutionary Vladimir Lenin. Rivera's didactic gesture — the choice that labor must make between socialism and barbarism — receives a new meaning. The capitalist will not even allow the worker to have that choice. Even the memory of that choice must be removed.

In contemporary art there is a crisis of auric value (the mutually reinforcing social and spiritual value of the work) — and the cultic performance that shapes it. At first this was driven by the apparent end of the modernist avant-garde telos (the succession of formal and conceptual innovations in art). It is now driven by a total digital installation that is larger than the art institution itself — a global capitalist participatory digital *gesamtkunstwerk or 'total work'*.[155] The concept of a total work — or gesamtkunstwerk — is related to Richard Wagner's popularization of the latter term, which he used in the production of his operas. The

---

154 Davis, *9.5 Theses on Art and Class*, 52-53.

155 I first made this argument in Turl, Adam "The Work of Art in the Age of Digital Reproduction," *Red Wedge Magazine* (May 1, 2019): http://www.redwedgemagazine.com/online-issue/digital-reproduction, based on Boris Groys' understanding of the Soviet Union as *Stalin Gesamtuknstwerk* in Groys, Boris, *The Total Art of Stalinism* (Verso, 2011).

idea, in essence, was to use several art forms — design, painting, music, lighting, sculpture — to immerse a patron within a "total artwork."

In *Stalin Gesamtkunstwerk*, Boris Groys argues that the "socialism" of the Soviet Union amounted, at least phenomenologically, to a total art installation in which public life became a sort of performance for the state.[156] In the contemporary US (at a minimum) the digital image has come to be part of its own total installation — a collective neoliberal performance. In the "Work of Art in the Age of Its Technological Reproducibility" (1936), Walter Benjamin writes that the (then) "function of film is to train human beings in the appreciations and reactions needed to deal with a vast apparatus whose role in their lives is expanding almost daily."[157] Social media and its digital images have a similar function. Whereas film conditioned the masses of industrial capitalism and sometimes sublimated left and right wing responses to its crises, the digital *gesamtkunstwerk* conditions the increasingly precarious masses of neoliberal capitalism and telegraphs nascent and weak socialist and fascist responses to its crises. The lessons it teaches, however, diverge from film. The montage element of film, by necessity, creates a unified totality determined by the filmmakers (actualized in the eye and mind of the viewer). The montage of the digital *gesamtkunstwerk* appears random and decontextualized, but is, as noted, determined by algorithms meant to maximize information and capital accumulation.[158]

---

156 Groys, *The Total Art of Stalinism*. The book's untranslated title is *Stalin Gesamtkunstwerk*.

157 Benjamin, *The Work of Art in the Age of Its Technological Reproducibility*, 37.

158 For an extreme (but now outdated) version of this dynamic see the phenomenon of algorithm-generated YouTube videos for children. "Random" characters (from Marvel, Disney, etc.) are generated based on view totals related to keywords (Spiderman, The Hulk, etc.). These are then put through plot generators, also based on data collection, and animations (and sometimes scripts for live actors) are produced. See Briddle, James, "How Peppa Pig Became a Video Nightmare for Children," *The Guardian* (June 17, 2018) and Maheshwari, Sapna "On YouTube Kids, Startling Videos Slip Past Filters," *The New York Times* (November 4, 2017): https://www.theguardian.com/technology/2018/jun/17/peppa-pig-youtube-weird-algorithms-automated-content and https://www.nytimes.com/2017/11/04/business/

The most capitalist film studios needed human directors and writers to shape the totality of a movie. This means that, even in Hollywood, critical and sometimes "socialist" films could be produced. The new meta-montage does not have a human director.[159] The final product is determined directly by capitalist algorithms. The remaining human element — in the vast digital artwork we all contribute to — tends to be concentrated in the production of isolated images and texts as they are put into montage, before they are given new association and meaning by the total installation of neoliberal capitalism.[160] But even *that* human element is threatened by generative AI. This floating image can take on a profoundly alienating character depending on its "random" re-contextualization into the world. An Instagram image of "food porn" on a tourist's smartphone walking through Times Square in Manhattan has a vastly different meaning than the very same image on the phone of a working-class single mother walking by the partial ruin of the River Rouge Complex in Detroit. The image is liberated but the spectator isn't. The digital *gesamtkunstwerk* becomes a constant reminder, in negative space, of social position. It is designed for ranking oneself in a vast neoliberal online role-playing game.[161]

We create our own doppelgangers and do so repeatedly. We, in

---

media/youtube-kids-paw-patrol.html.

159 As Toby Juliff and Travis Cox note there has been a tendency to ignore, in art and cultural theory, the actual coding of online space. Referring to Julian Stallabrass' *Internet Art: The Online Clash of Culture and Commerce*, they argue "the failure to specifiy the nature of that code — and in particular, in its relation to artist and user — in terms that challenge the privileged position of the interface, display and user, initiates further consideration…" Juliff, Toby and Cox, Travis, "The Post-display Condition of Contemporary Computer Art," emaj 8 (April 2015), 4: https://emajartjournal.files.wordpress.com/2012/11/cox-and-juliff_the-post-display-condition-of-contemporary-computer-art.pdf.

160 It is important to note that the Internet and the digital *gesamtkunstwerk* are not the same thing per se.

161 MMORPG stands for "massively multiplayer online role-playing game" — for example: *World of Warcraft*, *Guild Wars*, etc. These are video games that are played online with other players, usually with a strong role playing aspect.

a sense, perform how neoliberal capital sees the working-class, as an endlessly exchangeable multiplicity of supposedly "unique" (but always changing and reproducible) modules. We do this in a space in which each person/subject/worker is seemingly lifted from social context. The Horatio Alger myth is written into the structure of social media. Horatio Alger was a disgraced 19th century preacher who wrote novels about boys from modest or poor backgrounds who become rich through hard work, luck, and moxie. These tropes have permeated US culture. When we perform our digital selves, we largely *curate* ourselves. In this way Facebook, Instagram, TikTok and Twitter/X are the white cube writ large. But unlike the white cube exhibition space, which also valorizes the unique art object by underlining its auric value, the digital space eradicates auric value. We imagine we will become *more* with every post and image (but the inverse is usually true). We perform, in our online selves, a cultural echo of lean production (a management philosophy that aims at minimal input and maximum output), to prove we are the indispensable unit.

In this sense, when we (on the left) call out the avatars of our fellow working-class and oppressed siblings — usually but not always for "correct" leftist reasons — we are also re-enacting the competition enabled by lean production. A function of the digital image, as organized by capital's digital *gesamtkunstwerk*, is to map and commodify our dreams, to foster a neoliberalism of the soul.[162] Part of the work-

---

162 I am borrowing this phrase from the discussion/debate about the United Auto Workers (UAW) union failure to organize a Volkswagen plant in Chattanooga, Tennessee in 2013-2014. Richard Seymour wrote: "Union mishandling played a role in this, of which more in a moment. However, to grasp how they fucked up so badly, it is necessary to see how they were fighting on a terrain that was far more structurally loaded against them than they perhaps realized. The real question is not why unions fuck up in their bureaucratic, back-room way, but why workers were so available for the Right. This sort of outcome cries out for a neoliberalism-in-their-souls form of analysis.' Seymour, Richard, "Hegemony begins in the workplace," Lenin's Tomb (February 19, 2014): http://www.leninology.co.uk/2014/02/hegemony-be-

ing-class dream is the abolition of oppression and exploitation. In this way, the digital call out can easily become an anti-working-class manifestation of a working-class dream.[163]

This totalizing installation — existing in almost every aspect of contemporary life — reshapes the cultic performance of the art space itself. The critical potential of installation art is that it can act as a *counter-totality* — a counter-narrative — to this ideological *gesamtkunstwerk*. At the same time, installation art can also be another iteration or element within the total art of capitalism.[164]

THE ORGANIZATION OF CULTIC PERFORMANCE

As Walter Benjamin notes, "the contextual integration of art in tradition found its expression in the cult" — a more or less permanent siting in the church, in temples, buildings of state, and its relations to those performances of church and state. "Artistic production begins with ceremonial objects," Benjamin argues. The meanings of devotional images, a handmade book of hours and the icon, were bound spatially and conceptually to social ritual, sculpting the *distance* between viewer and image/object. As art patronage shifted from church to the bourgeois individual, and easel painting became a craft industry in every European city and town, cult-value was, according to Benjamin, shifted to "exhibition value."[165] This eventually produced the salon; a jumbled market of images and objects for sale, reflecting the political economy of easel painting as a boutique market.[166] This did not yet reflect a

gins-in-workplace.html.

163 The digital "call out" became one of the most problematic aspects of online left culture. Most of the criticisms of the "call out," however, quickly degenerated into minimizing oppressions. This, of course, completes the ideological job of capital coming and going.

164 It is important to note that the Internet and the digital *gesamtkunstwerk* are not the same thing per se.

165 Benjamin, *The Work of Art in the Age of Its Technological Reproducibility*, 26 and John Berger, *Ways of Seeing* (Penguin, 1972).

166 Berger, *Ways of Seeing*, 83-106.

coherent bourgeois ideology. That took shape with the advent of the modernist "white cube" wherein each "individual" artwork, separated from economic and social context, became a unique object of "genius" floating in space.[167]

We must note, however, that the salon and white cube are/were also *cultic performances* of the art object. The nature of the placement of the artworks and their organized interactions with patrons communicate meaning that is then re-embedded into the unique object. The public museum reflected both bourgeois ideology and a democratic ideal. Art objects acted as both commodity fetishes and artistic fetishes.[168] The modernist canonical art space was a contradiction; elevating individual subjectivity in a positivist manner — dead subjectivity pinned to the wall like butterflies. It was these contradictions that Ilya and Emelia Kabakov attempted to exploit in their "total installations," manipulating "auracity"[169] to create narrative meaning for *constrained subjects* through the secular and sacral aspects of the art space.

Many modern artists had some consciousness of the intermixing of cultic and exhibition value — although it was sometimes an intuitive intervention. Notable for us — as Marxists in an irrealist tradition — are the Berlin Dada Art Fair of 1920, and the Paris Surrealist Exhibition of 1938. Each of these assaulted the positivism of the bourgeois exhibition space — *re-enchanting relations between discrete elements* and *re-asserting social relationships between those elements*. In Berlin, Dadaist slogans in solidarity with the German Revolution and workers movement were scrawled on the wall, a German soldier's uniform was placed on a dummy with a pig's mask and hung from the ceiling, while paintings, photographs, and assemblages surrounded it. The sculpture with a pig

---

167 Radoshovich, "Zombie Gallery."
168 See Adorno on the dual nature of the art commodity/fetish.
169 Kabakov, Ilya, Tupitsyn, Margarita, and Tupitsyn, Victor, "About Installation," *Art Journal* Vol. 58 No. 4 (Winter 1999), 65 and Koenig, Wendy, "The Heroic Generation: Fictional Socialist Realist Painters in the Work of Ilya Kabakov," *Southwestern Art Conference Review* Vol. 10, Issue 4 (2009), 448-455.

mask, titled *Prussian Archangel*, was made by John Heartfield and Rudolf Schlicter, and resulted in criminal charges against the artists. In the 1938 Paris exhibition, coal bags stuffed with newspaper were hung from the ceiling in dimly lit rooms — which meant patrons had to strain their eyes to see the works as coal dust drifted above their heads, dry leaves covered the floor, and a web of string crossed artworks. Criticality and marvelousness — in a Surrealist sense — were constructed.

Two things should be noted/underlined. In both cases, the patronage/viewership was largely bourgeois and middle-class, albeit relatively diverse within those limits (German expatriates in Paris, déclassé aristocratic refugees, various outcasts, etc.). While the Berlin exhibition got Heartfield and Schlicter arrested (they were later acquitted), the Paris exhibit was a "smash hit." This is not a criticism. It is noted because, since the modernist project has waned, the class nature of the art audience has become a bigger part of the *meaning of art itself*. A well-heeled audience in 1938 meant very little to the then-perceived meaning of the work. The bourgeois nature of the audience has taken on a different meaning following art's fusion with finance capital and gentrification on a global level. Nevertheless, the Berlin and Paris exhibitions challenged modes of bourgeois art exhibition on both social and existential terms. Ongoing attacks on bourgeois modes of art installation were woven throughout the happenings of the 1960s. Fluxus, the works of Joseph Beuys, the idea of conceptual art as a "dematerialization of the art object," in Arte Povera's installation of "poor materials," etc. As Lippard notes of dematerialization, the attempt to escape the commodity form was unsuccessful over time. Eventually, even overtly "political" art-world art was defanged of its critical, revolutionary or Marxist character.[170]

---

170 Plant, Sadie, *The Most Radical Gesture: The Situationist International in a Post-Modern Age* (Routledge, 1992), 111-112. See also Adam Turl, "Against the Weak Avant-Garde," *Red Wedge* (April 5, 2016): http://www.redwedgemagazine.com/online-issue/weak-avant-garde.

SOCIAL PRACTICE ART

If the art space can become, in a Brechtian sense, a theatrical space, do the artworks become "flats" (large paintings used to establish settings on stage) for theatrical action? What is the action? How is cult value performed? This raises questions of social practice art and relational aesthetics. As noted with Claire Bishop's criticisms, social practice art tends to reproduce bourgeois ideology. An "installation" in which artists distribute food to upper middle-class Brooklynites simply reinforces gentrification and the displacement of workers and people of color while appearing to be "social."[171] The artist Rirkirit Tiravanija, for example, frequently organizes performances and installations in which he cooks food for people. As Bishop argues, in relation to a Tiravanija performance in New York, the *social* aspect of this performance became, in large part, art world insiders — critics, curators, collectors — gossiping about the "art world" over food in an art gallery instead of a restaurant.[172] It is hard to see how this is more "radically social" than the "detached opticality" of historic artifacts like Picasso's *Guernica* or Rivera's *Man at the Crossroads*. As discussed, Picasso's *Guernica* (1937) was a large (mostly) grisaille painting made in response to the Nazi bombardment of a Spanish town during the Spanish Civil War. The painting was toured, at one point, to raise funds for the Spanish Republicans. Diego Rivera's *Man at the Crossroads* (1933) is a re-creation of a mural he had painted at Rockefeller Center in New York City. The point here is that the social performance around these works — war, censorship, resistance, and so on — has imbued them with critical auric meaning.

Of course, there are instances of social practice art and relational aesthetics that have overcome this problem. For example, see Thomas Hirschhorn's *Gramsci Monument* (2013) in the Forest Houses

---

171 Bishop, *Artificial Hells*, 25-26.
172 Bishop, Claire, "Art of the Encounter: Antagonism and Relational Aesthetics," *Circa* No. 114 (Winter 2005), 33.

public housing estate in the Bronx, or the artistic gestures of Félix González-Torres. One of the ways these works tended to avoid the problem identified by Bishop was by creating a *collaboration* of *radical* meaning. The *Gramsci Monument* provided communicative and other resources for a working-class community while seeming to avoid complicity with gentrification. The overdetermination of its aesthetics was limited to the DIY ethos of its structure, the mural of Gramsci painted on plywood outside, etc. The main meaning of the work came in its provision of computer access and other services to the neighborhood. Felix González-Torres's minimalist inspired "take a candy" pieces recuperated meaning that had been eradicated from dematerialized aesthetics. The individual candies become something like transubstantiated eucharists, democratized in the volume of their tragic being and their association with the AIDS crisis.

RELATIONAL AESTHETICS AS CRISIS

In hindsight, the broader popularity of Nicolas Bourriaud's version of relational aesthetics prefigured a general crisis of the canonical art space. Bourriaud's erratic 1998 book, *Relational Aesthetics*, struggles with the shifting meaning of the unique art experience/object at the end of the 20th century. While recognizing that the "viewer" has become an "intrinsic part" of the art, (hence the 'relational' aspect), he conflates the meaning of Benjaminian *aura* with "the public."[173] The viewer/patron had always been central in Benjaminian aura. At relational aesthetics' core, however, is less a shift in the responsibility or involvement of the audience vs. artist, but a shift in the point of view of *art space administration* — away from the art space as a repository of "art for art's sake" toward art space as *attraction or entertainment* presented as a kind of social laboratory.

Bourriaud argues against the white cube sans the radical politics

---

173 Bourriaud, Nicolas, *Relational Aesthetics* (Les Presses Du Reel, 1998), 58-59.

that historically critiqued it. Claiming the mantle of Berlin Dada (1919) and Paris Surrealism (1938), art museums are presented as open "works in progress" in themselves. They promise an ostensible democracy of activity within the art space, and to leave the social whole outside. Instead of challenging bourgeois ideology, relational art has brought the museum's artistic contents into alignment with the values of neoliberal capitalism, as opposed to capital's earlier values of "art for art's sake." This process later produced the depoliticized and decontextualized spectacles of digitized Van Gogh immersions and Meow Wolf theme parks.[174] Instead of telegraphing "future utopias," Bishop argues that such work creates "micro-utopias."[175] As the patrons who participate in these relational aesthetic experiences are mostly petit-bourgeois and bourgeois persons who *already live in their own utopias*, it recreates semi-private Elysiums within the art space. It also prefigures the social media subject, who is conditioned to convey false realities and then meet those realities when they leave the house. In this sense, relational art must today be, above-all, worthy of photographing and posting on social media.

Bishop argues of the majority of relational aesthetic artists cited by Bourriaud, that, "[r]ather than forming a coherent and distinctive transformation of space [in the manner of 'total installation,' a theatrical mise-en-scene]...' they "insist upon *use* rather than contemplation."[176] This individuated use is a direct contradiction of both romantic and modern conceptions of art that held out art's *lack of utilitarian purpose* or art's universal utopian purpose.[177] There is a long-standing left and utopian desire to "activate" the audience (in Dada and Fluxus happenings, in Beuysian practice, in Brechtian theater). However, most social practice

174 Bishop, Claire, "Antagonism and Relational Aesthetics," *October* 110 (Autumn 2004), 54-55.
175 Bishop, "Antagonism and Relational Aesthetics," 55.
176 Bishop, "Antagonism and Relational Aesthetics," 56.
177 Bishop, "Antagonism and Relational Aesthetics," 58.

art produces a kind of "ubiquitous polysemic reification," a *reduction* of social relationships to the level of service or storefront experience, i.e. *"literal interactions."*[178] It creates a social version of the tautophrase. There is no moral outrage or decision to be made. It is what it is. It avoids the gothic churn of time.

The antidote to this problem is the *consciously participatory* rather than passive (read: ideological) construction of the cultic. Bishop writes, "at its best, delegated performance produces disruptive events that testify to a *shared reality* between viewers and performers..."[179] It is an open question how this might relate to cybernetic and digital spaces. On the one hand most people — at least in industrialized countries — actively and regularly participate in digital spaces. However, this is not necessarily conscious, and it is shaped in the last instance by capital. The digital seems activated by the gothic largely in negative space. It glows on the ruins around it. At the same time, repeating digital enclosures (corporate and state), along with the passage of time and IRL disasters, have begun to create a gothic and auric Internet.[180]

As noted in the opening of this book, the term gothic refers here, as it does in much academic literature, to the contradictory confrontation of the contemporary or new with the archaic or anachronistic. In art and literature, the gothic — the ruin, the old mansion, the rustic countryside — is often presented as both nostalgia and threat, seductive and repulsive, alien but familiar. It was US government resources that created the early Internet. And it was US industrialism that enabled postwar American global hegemony. But much of industrial America and the early promise of the Internet lays in ruin.

---

178 Bishop, "Antagonism and Relational Aesthetics," 62.
179 Bishop, Claire, "Delegated Performance: Outsourcing Authenticity," *October* (Spring 2021), 112.
180 For my purposes here I schematize Internet culture in three stages: Arpanet/classical Internet (1970s - 1990s), open/anarchic Internet (1994-2000) and the increasingly enclosed Internet (after 2001).

The relatively open/anarchic phase of the Internet (which continued with ever-decreasing efficacy after 2001) created a new constellation of referents and signs that contain particular meanings for the formative generation that suffered the traumas of the War on Terror (2001-) and the economic crisis (2008-). *This was the Internet before the fall.* Many became generational-cultural reference points; the LOSS meme (2008-) for example, and some, like the web series *Don't Hug Me I'm Scared* (2011-2016), are impressive works of art. Alternative reality games (ARGs) and trans media storytelling (TMS) — before their rapid co-optation by marketing departments — offered new models for critical narratives. Primitive Internet graphics (associated with platforms like GeoCities) have taken on an increasingly gothic hue. All recall a narrowed digital idyll. As people die and their avatars remain online, in the future the majority of avatars in the digital *gesamtkunstwerk* will be avatars of the dead. Moreover, there is the conspiracy theory called "Dead Internet" which holds that there are very few "real people" online anymore and that individuals mostly interact with AIs and bots.

WE ARE ALL OUTSIDERS NOW[181]

The concept of outsider art, or self-taught art, is a lie. It conceals the actual artistic arguments and content articulated by the artists described in this way. While the history of the concept is complicated, its present usage is bound up with a racial, class and geographic othering which centers the bourgeois and petit-bourgeois institutional art world as the norm (when it is itself the outlier). Unlike the genealogy of abstraction, performance, conceptual art or installation art, the genealogy of outsider, self-taught, or "folk art," traces less the lineage of art and artists, and maps the evolution of the concept itself. The history of outsider art is a history of categorization.

As part of the modern art impulse to search out expressive inputs

---

181 Based on articles posted on the *Red Wedge* site in 2019.

beyond the sclerotic academic art canon, 19th and early 20th century artists looked to folk arts, the arts of the European colonies and the art of "marginalized" or supposedly "pure" actors, such as the mentally insane or children. These impulses were contradictory. On the one hand, artists were correct in seeking inputs to rebel against the old aesthetic order. On the other hand, European artists often misunderstood what they were looking at, particularly in the case of "non-western" art, reading it through an orientalist lens. The least problematic of these appropriations were undertaken by consciously political artists who borrowed from folk, religious, and popular traditions in their own communities and areas of geographic origin, with specific aesthetic and political goals in mind.

Two figures key to the history of "outsider art" are Jean Dubuffet and the surrealist André Breton.

Breton's surrealism, influenced by Freudian psychoanalysis and Marxism, sought social excavations of the subconscious. Some surrealists viewed the art of the mentally ill, children, and non-western artists as closer to the subconscious, and therefore, liberation. A case can be made for this idea regarding the art of children. But the idea that non-western artists, or the mentally ill, are inherently primitive, is obviously problematic at best.[182] While the Surrealists were consistently anti-imperialist, their hatred of bourgeois European civilization could reproduce aspects of western chauvinism. European chauvinism read colonized persons as less advanced. The surrealist response was sometimes to celebrate a perceived primitiveness. The assumption that the art of long-standing (non-European) civilizations and class-societies was closer to the ("good") "primitive" could be seen as an inversion

---

182 For a good exposition of the tension of surrealist and other European avant-gardes to this question see Conley, Katharine, "Surrealism and Outsider Art: From the 'Automatic Message' to André Breton's Collection." *Yale French Studies*, no. 109 (2006): 129–43. For an early exposition of this dynamic from Breton see Breton, Andre "The Automatic Message," *Minotaure* No. 3-4 (Paris, 1933).

of racist ideology.

More important to the present-day art-world marketing of "outsider" art is the legacy of Jean Dubuffet. Dubuffet promoted, in far simpler terms than Breton, the art of "outsiders," the mentally ill, children, etc., under his rubric of "Art Brut." While he emphasized such work's "rawness, spontaneity, and individuality" he also insisted that to be categorized as such, an artist must be "socially isolated and exercise his or her creativity in complete isolation from external cultural influences."[183] This is obviously not possible. First of all, even Roger Cardinal, who coined the term "outsider art," observes the importance of scavenging (images, objects, etc.) by the artists in question. Such a practice literally incorporates "external" influences. As James Elkins argues, the very idea of "outsider art" is an oxymoron.[184] Art was born alongside the rise of social consciousness in hunter-gatherer societies. While self-expression is an important aspect of art, so too is its social genesis and reception. There can be no art in "complete isolation from external cultural influences."

In the United States, the modernist impulse to look outside the historic art academy was found in a focus on American "folk art." In the 1930s the Museum of Modern Art (MoMA) organized two exhibitions of folk art curated by Holger Cahill. As Eugene Metcalf argues, "[f]olk art served to connect to artists of the twenties and thirties with a long tradition apparently unique to America, giving them not only historical and cultural roots but also a reply to the critics of modern art who claimed it was only another version of decadent European civilization."[185]

Metcalf argues in the essay "Black Art, Folk Art, and Social Con-

---

183 Davies, David, "On the Very Idea of 'Outsider Art,'" *British Journal of Aesthetics* 49 (January 2009), 26.

184 Davies, "On the Very Idea of 'Oustider Art,'" 27.

185 Metcalf, Eugene W., "Black Art, Folk Art, and Social Control," *Winterthur Portfolio* Vol. 18 No. 4 (Winter 1983), 278.

trol," that the mainstream art world, in historic folk exhibitions and in the Corcoran Gallery of Art's famous 1982 exhibit, "Black Folk Art in America," flattened and decontextualized the meaning of the artists and artworks. Due to class and racial prejudices, albeit in their liberal form, work by poor, working-class, Black, southern and rural artists was read as closer to nature, as primitive, as mysterious and unknowable, or the continuation of lost craft culture (in the case of working-class and rural white artists), or the elaboration of a pure primitive African art (in the case of Black artists).[186] Art was presented this way even when there was substantial contradictory evidence.

The artist Bill Traylor, an elderly African American man, born a slave, was "discovered" in the 1940s by a liberal white middle-class southerner named Charles Shannon. Shannon recognized the importance of Traylor's work, collected and promoted it. But it never occurred to Shannon to ask Traylor what his work was about, what his motivations were, what he was chronicling in thousands of drawings. Now, decades later, academics more or less try to guess what the work was about. The significance of Traylor's work is ascribed the dubious honor of authenticity; but an authenticity without agency; or an "unknowable" agency deemed somehow less conscious or deliberate than, say, a thousand polka dot paintings from Damien Hirst. For example, Traylor frequently drew large dogs towering over human beings. These fantastic beasts evoke the dogs used to hound slaves and later free Black persons in the US south.

Or take the work of William Thompson. The (barely) concealed anti-Semitism and right-wing lunacy of his art is almost actively hidden by art collectors, dealers and writers in awe of his southern gothic authenticity and marketability.[187] These works are colorful and schematic, like medieval topographies of the cosmos or heaven and hell. They mix

---

186 Metcalf, "Black Art, Folk Art," 271-289.
187 For an accounting of this work, as well as other work, see Bottoms, Greg, *The Colorful Apocalypse: Journeys in Outsider Art* (University of Chicago Press, 2007), 57-121.

images and texts. And to be fair, if one approaches them as only aesthetic patterns, one might miss their reactionary political aspects. But they are not *all that* hidden. In one painting there is a text that reads, "The Great Deception of Church and State." At the top of the painting the numbers "666" and the words "New World Order... Empire of Satan" are depicted. The surface of the painting is crossed with something that looks like a Star of David. This "Star of David" motif repeats in other works and is associated with some kind of spiritual or social evil.

Ralph Fasanella, a working-class union organizer turned artist is described as "self-taught" even though the content of his work reflects the lessons of decades of class struggle. Moreover, through his union, Ralph Fasanella organized art classes at city college for himself and other members. He spent a great deal of time studying works in New York museums. His aesthetic training is made clear in his subtle uses of color and form. Most of his paintings show cityscapes or crowds. In many cityscapes, the buildings and architecture are mostly cool blues and greens, punctuated by warm yellows and other colors. In other works, he makes didactic remarks with text and more overtly political images — figures on strike, words summarizing his opposition to imperialism. This is not naïve work.

That is not to say there is not a genuine appeal in work that has been categorized as "outsider." The appeal of much of this so-called outsider art is that it, unlike the art world proper, aims to speak largely to audiences outside the art world, embraces individual artistic subjectivity, and presents a totality, a complete philosophical world vision, at a time when the majority of the art world has been trained to avoid such visions. Moreover, this totality is often expressed in opposition to the perceived status quo, albeit it in a frequently esoteric and sometimes a right-wing manner.

But we can only learn from this art if we treat it as genuine conscious work. It arrives organically — but consciously — from social contexts outside the "art world" proper. In this way, the work can have a greater proximity to a gothic-futurist working-class subject. Thompson's apocalyptic paintings provide a reactionary explanation for the social-existential crisis. Traylor's drawings preserve images — real and dream-like — from the struggle against the racist horrors of US history. Fasanella freezes working-class New York — a city that has since been gentrified as no other — as a fluid glow. These works were born in ruins.

Abstractions of 'authenticity' and 'otherness' conceal and reify what this work actually means, good or bad, and preserve market shares for different currents of artistic commodities.

This is part of a wider historical process. The avant-garde, which had an oppositional role aesthetically, and sometimes politically in the 19th and 20th centuries, moved away from expressionism, "metanarratives," and totality, while, at the same time, becoming more and more open to capital. To be sure, art institutions had always been tied to money and corruption. But as long as the innovating dynamics of modern art remained important, the cultured bourgeois had to tolerate, at least to some degree, the anarchism and socialism of (some of) its artists.

Despite platitudes and token gestures towards social art, the dominant ruling-class modern art ideology was "art for art's sake." Postmodernism tore down this ideology, but not in favor of the political. In the 1980s and 1990s this was presented, in part, as a progressive dismantling of dominant white male narratives — and to some degree it was. But after the art world stripped art of its bourgeois social-spiritual use value it replaced it with… nothing. Art became, without a reason for being, increasingly utilitarian. Pretense aside, the new mandarins of art remained mostly white, rich, and male. Artists concerned with individual subjectivity and social totality were evicted from the art world. Social criticism was possible, even desirable, but so long as it only went so far. Moreover, the art had to be saleable.

Squeezed between immiseration and new technology, the art market has become polarized — not in a useful political sense — like retail more generally. On the one hand there are pedestrian art fairs and Etsy, and on the other, high-end galleries and international art fairs. Etsy is an online marketplace for arts and crafts, in which artists can sell their work online. The platform, in exchange, receives a percentage of the sale. The mid-range galleries, often the bedrock of modernist experimentation, are going out of business. The top of the art world has become increasingly meshed with finance capital. Writing of the contemporary art market, Rachel Wetzler observes:

> As contemporary art is increasingly viewed as an asset
> class – alongside equities, bonds, and real estate… art
> works [are] often used as a vehicle to hide or launder
> money, and artists encouraged to churn out works in
> market-approved styles, bringing about a decline in
> quality.[188]

At street level, the art world is more and more complicit in gentrification. As cities have deindustrialized, local politicians have sought ways to economically diversify and repurpose urban spaces. While gentrification predates the 1964 coining of the term it has become increasingly important in US urban policy, as has its relationship to art. Art institutions, starved for money since the decimation of federal funding in the 1990s, turned to opportunistic funds from real estate and financial capital, as well as gentrifying local governments. Artists, although largely unpaid for the service, add aesthetic value to urban spaces, allowing real estate interests to price out working-class residents, and, ultimately, most artists.

The art world is increasingly tied to finance capital, complicit in gentrification, ideologically hostile to individual subjective expression and collective emancipation, materially inhospitable to the work-

---

188 Wetzler, Rachel, "How Modern Art Serves the Rich," *The New Republic* (February 26, 2018).

ing-class, to most women and people of color, practically inaccessible to poor, working-class, and even many middle-class persons. In many cases it is abusive to the working-class people already a part of it. The contemporary art world is even wary of the modern bourgeois idea of art, not to mention Romantic and pre-capitalist conceptions of art. In effect, the ideology, structure and economy of the weak avant-garde has made most of us outsiders.

Academically trained working-class artists who pretend their hard-earned knowledge, BFAs and MFAs, make them immune to this dynamic are fooling themselves. It is understandable. We do not want to think of ourselves as art world dark-matter, permanent adjuncts, and stalking horses for gentrification. But this is what the art world is making of us, and what we must break from as workers, as artists, and as socialists.

Outsider art is not closer to the subconscious. However, much of the work categorized as such does emphasize, to a much greater degree than contemporary institutional art, the importance of individual subjectivity and self-expression. By categorizing individual expression as naïve, quaint and outsider, the art world can commodify this expression while still embracing a post-human and technology-fetishizing contemporary art. Working-class expression, however, is alien to the bourgeoisie. It is, by definition, truly "outside" the realm of bourgeois cultural exchange[189]

For working class artists, embracing our "outsiderness" holds the promise of developing a constituency for experimental art beyond the institutional art world. This promise, however, would likely be short-circuited by the way in which outsider art is generally incorporated into the art world; denying or minimizing the agency of artists, minimizing

---

189 What might be called "outsider" work on the Internet, however, seems to be marginalized less by ideological argument than algorithm. Every successful shitpost or critical meme seems to produce, eventually, a further enclosure — a further tightening of the algorithm.

the specificity of context (beyond biographies that exaggerate otherness), and often obscuring the content of work.

Outsider art tends to emphasize content; even when that content is obscurantist, theological, or conspiratorial. The weak avant-garde tends to minimize content. Therefore, the art world, starved for anything that actually says something, reifies outsider art. The *form* of saying something is celebrated. What is actually said must be, at least partially, *hidden*. This may be because an individual artist is a fundamentalist Christian lunatic. Or they may be an uncompromising throwback to the old left. Either way, the institutional art world, like the neoliberal political center, cannot really fathom these things in the concrete.

Many outsider artists engage in world-building. They present a counter-narrative to the world as is. This may or may not be progressive, intentionally "political," and may be reactionary. But these artists present a totalizing mythology. The art world has been trained to disbelieve such things. This disbelief makes it much easier for the artifacts of the weak avant-garde to be incorporated into the art market *and* the totalizing mythologies of neoliberal capital. Many outsider artists, by contrast, have a mission. Indeed, this is part of their great appeal in an art world that has been trained by school and conditioned by capitalist realism to be suspicious of larger purposes. Something can be learned from them, despite the difficulty in surmounting the obstacle of the bourgeois art market.

LESSONS FROM OUTSIDE

1) Individual subjective expression remains important. Far from being bourgeois, it can be, in its very form, an argument against a depersonalizing post-human contemporary capitalist culture. 2) Socialist artists should aim to develop, by the content of their work, and its geography and social orientation, constituencies beyond the art world. Indeed, these should come first, before the art world. 3) While working class art need not always be didactic, it should embrace an overdetermined

and unapologetic socialism. This is much easier, of course, after the artist decides the art world is not their primary audience. 4) The working-class artist should take from so-called outsider art its tendency towards the construction of mythologies. Building myths will focus on the intersection of the subjective individual with collective emancipation; the existential and the social.

THE IMMORTALITY OF THINGS

An important layer of academic art historians and curators have a vested interest in maintaining the weak echo of modernist essentialism or jettisoning it for a neoliberal relativism. As the priests of art they are the keepers of an incomprehensible "word." The art market, despite being dominated by the mega-galleries, contains some well-meaning gallery owners. Regardless, the system depends on the sale of work. This commodification does not change the fact of the gallery's theatricality but complicates its conscious use; undermining art and the social and existential conditions art needs to address. The theatricality of relational aesthetics and social practice art often recreates — in what was a potentially critical idiom — more spectacle. Artificial Intelligence image generators and digital art further threaten the philosophical-materiality of art with what Ben Davis calls a crisis of substitutability.[190] Moreover, as Groys argues, "the museum is, by definition, opposed to progress for it is the place dedicated to the immortality of things."[191] The goal must not be to stop the museum's dedication to immortality, but to replace the word "things" with "people:" *the billions of unique subjectivities repressed by the global anti-narrative of neoliberal capital.* This includes "things" in as much as they are a record of a (very temporal) human performance.

---

190 Davis, *Art in the After-Culture.*
191 Groys, *Ilya Kabakov,,* 15.

4: A DIGITAL BOOK OF HOURS[192]

The Total Society Has Become—Cyborgs in Crises—
Barbenheimer—The social-subjectivity of Marxism—Social
Sublime—The Capitalist Book of Hours

In the Middle Ages, books of hours were hand-made devotional prayer books. They contained within them psalms and prayers and were illuminated by drawings. The books were meant to be used at specific times throughout the day. They were often smaller than other hand-produced books. They provided a kind of intimate solace for the believer at regular intervals. They were not completely unlike the small digital screens we carry with us today.

In Sam Esmail's liberal-apocalyptic film, *Leave the World Behind* (2023), the United States suffers a series of cyberattacks that produce power outages, shut down the Internet and phone services, shipwreck oil tankers, and cause airplanes to fall from the sky. At one-point, self-driving Tesla automobiles create a massive pile-up on the highway. Those behind the cyberattacks are not disclosed in the film. Instead, the film focuses on the personal responses of a family from Brooklyn vacationing in a rented house on Long Island when the attacks begin — and on the family that rented them the house. The vacationing couple, Amanda and Clay Sandford (Julia Roberts and Ethan Hawke), and their two kids, Archie and Rose (Charlie Evans and Farrah Mackenzie), are thrown onto a metaphorical life raft with the father who rented them the home, G.H. Scott (Mahershala Ali) and his daughter, Ruth (Myha'la).

Several cybernetic questions are raised by the film. When the movie begins, Rose, the Sandford's thirteen-year-old daughter, has been binge-watching the sitcom *Friends* (1994). The cyber-attacks occur as

---

192 This chapter incorporates material from various articles written for *Locust Review*, *Imago*, and the author's academic work.

she is about to stream the *Friends* series finale. As the world — or at least the United States — collapses into chaos and civil war, Rose is frustrated that she is unable to watch the finale. In the final scene of the film, Rose stumbles upon a wealthy family's doomsday bunker. The bunker has electricity and a massive supply of DVDs. She, of course, decides to watch the *Friends* finale. The show's theme-song plays over the closing credits.[193] In much of the critical discourse on the cybernetic, there is concern of about the obliteration of the self, the end of human subjectivity. In *Leave the World Behind*, when Rose presses play on the *Friends* DVD, Ruth and Amanda have just witnessed — from a distance — several large explosions in New York City. As the world comes unraveled, Rose takes refuge in a banal television show. It is, of course, understandable escapism. But there is also something greater linking mortality and the cybernetic; something that raises death and possibility of escaping death. This is because the cybernetic asks us where one's subjectivity ends and media/technology begins.

In David Cronenberg's *Videodrome* (1983), the main character, Max Renn (James Woods), exposed to a program called *Videodrome*, grows a tumor in his head that causes what seem to be televisual hallucinations, in what Mark Fisher describes as an "almost emblematic staging of the convergence of cybernetic and Gothic themes."[194] Max's mutation embodies a legitimate fear (currently exploited in "real life" hysterias around vaccine microchips, DNA resequencing and 5G cell phone tower conspiracies). The professor character in *Videodrome*, Dr. Brian O'Blivion — who believes that television is rapidly supplanting reality — Fisher argues, is a stand-in for the theorists Jean Baudrillard and Marshall McLuhan.[195] The show that infects Max Renn is essentially a

---

193 The film itself, while well made, has very liberal politics. It was produced, bizarrely, by Barack and Michelle Obama.
194 Fisher, Mark *Flatline Constructs* (Exmilitary, 2018), 71. The following paragraphs are based on earlier research and papers produced in my doctoral studies at SIUC.
195 Fisher, *Flatline Constructs*, 72-73.

snuff-film/tv series (developed as a sort of cybernetic weapon), echoing McLuhan on the "'curious fusion of sex, technology and death' in media artifacts."[196] Renn initially becomes interested in this "snuff-film"/TV show for business reasons. He is the head of an independent television channel in Toronto. He is attracted to the production, in part, because of its seemingly very low production costs. It is reality television, in effect, prefiguring the stripped-down media of the future century. The film ends with a series of Phillip K. Dick-like "reality loops" making its conclusion very difficult to trust, echoing the hallucinations of the main character.[197]

Max Renn's apocalypse is a personal one. The apocalypse facing the Scotts and Sandfords is wider. Each relates, however, to cybernetic anxiety. As Fisher argues, in JG Ballard's writing, the "distinction between inner and outer" is dissolved but "not in favor of interiority." This is, Fisher notes, a "reversal of Promethean SF." Fire is no longer wrested from the gods. Something has gone wrong. We cannot dominate the environment because we are part of the landscape and "bodies are themselves landscapes."[198] A wall between subject and object has fallen.

Does the almost sexual ecstasy of "ceasing to exist" by being absorbed into the cybernetic "stream" or "flow"[199] anesthetize us from unfolding apocalyptic disasters (pandemic, climate change)? Does the glowing sky on fire become, in our cybernetic minds, an Instagram filter? At the same time, the cybernetic seems to hold out the promise of a world without material constraint, a world of abundance. The augmentation of bodies should allow greater freedom in terms of gender as well as in life-saving medical services. The COVID-19 vaccines were dependent on complex computer software. The digital *should* ease the creation of a world without material constraint for the vast majority of

---

196 Fisher, *Flatline Constructs,* 72-73.
197 Fisher, *Flatline Constructs,* 73-74.
198 Fisher, *Flatline Constructs,* 85.
199 Fisher, *Flatline Constructs,* 18.

the human race.

As an artist, I have been obsessed with the overgrowth of digital imagery for more than a decade. What does it mean to make art in a world of seemingly endless viral reproducing digital images — *and* growing social crises and existential threats? In the early 2010s, I started burying my own work in a series I called *Dead Paintings*. I would leave them in the ground, usually for a period of eight months, and then exhume them and display their rotten corpses. When I transitioned back into making work that was not meant to be destroyed — in the mid-2010s— I started with paintings that I considered to be "anti-memes." I coupled text and images in a manner similar to the then ubiquitous meme formats circulating online, albeit heavily influenced by expressionism, art history, and a sense of (not particularly memetic) social and individual pathos. Re-reading Walter Benjamin, Bertolt Brecht, and Boris Groys, among others, I started to think about the totality of digital images; how they are combined in a kind of meta-montage by social media and streaming services. I started to think of that meta-montage as an artwork itself that reshaped the meaning of the discrete images placed within it. One vast sprawling work. Because that larger montage was determined and shaped by capitalist economics and ideology, I suspected we needed to begin to think of a kind of *counter*-montage.

THE TOTAL SOCIETY HAS BECOME

> The more total society becomes, the greater the reification of the mind and the more paradoxical its effort to escape reification on its own. Even the most extreme consciousness of doom threatens to degenerate into idle chatter. Cultural criticism finds itself faced with the final stage of the dialectic of culture and barbarism. To write poetry after Auschwitz is barbaric. And this corrodes even the knowledge of why it has become impossible to write poetry today. Absolute reification, which presupposed intellectual progress as

one of its elements, is now preparing to absorb the mind entirely. Critical intelligence cannot be equal to this challenge as long as it confines itself to self-satisfied contemplation. - Adorno, "Cultural Criticism and Society" (1949)[200]

In our "official culture" — including its social media and streaming — doom is often idle chatter, or "doom-scrolling".[201] Various apocalypses and dystopias have become clichéd entertainment — as if to make redundant Walter Benjamin's note on alienated humanity experiencing "its own destruction as an aesthetic pleasure of the first order."[202] The material "base" and the cultural "superstructure" have become — in tandem —"too much" for the artistic and political subject. The left (and the working-class and oppressed overall) continue to fail in cohering — or imagining — a counter-totality to Adorno's "total that society has become;" or an alternative to what Mark Fisher called, with different emphases and at a different historical conjuncture, "capitalist realism".[203] There are many important gestures at counter-imaginations — both "in real life" (IRL) and online. But, as individual elements, they often become a constituent part of much larger capitalist montages, spaces, and economies, which can shift or subdue their meanings.

It would seem axiomatic that the Holocaust would not have been possible in a world with smartphones or mass digital media, but what if there is a version of the world in which it would be possible *despite* (or even partially because of) mass digital media? We had video, photo-

---

200 Adorno, Theodor, *Prisms*, (MIT Press, 1983), 34.

201 Doom-scrolling is usually taken to mean spending an excessive amount of time scrolling through news and social media feeds, reading or skimming "bad news" repeatedly. However, some people take doom scrolling to refer to the act of mindlessly scrolling the feed itself, regardless of content.

202 Benjamin, Walter, "The Work of Art in the Age...", 42. I am quoting, however, the earlier draft of the essay posted at Marxists.org: https://www.marxists.org/reference/subject/philosophy/works/ge/benjamin.htm.

203 Fisher, Mark, *Capitalist Realism: Is There No Alternative* (Zero Books, 2009).

graphic, and textual access to the unnecessary mass deaths of millions due to COVID-19 and it happened anyway.[204] Or consider the problem of the weather as it relates to climate change. Timothy Morton argues that the most banal of all conversations becomes either a denial of climate disaster or another public acknowledgement of climate disaster. But, unlike a scab or a racist, you cannot punch the weather in the nose. You can't have a sit-in at the weather's office. You can't usually protest the meteorologist. Every time someone brings up the "weather" you are now reminded of the gap between what must be done and your own subjective capacity.

This is another aspect of the contradiction of participation in communicative capitalism.[205] On the one hand, to develop an informed war of position (in the Gramscian sense — the equivalent of today's "soft power") or war of maneuver (the decisive violent attack that Gramsci attributed to Leninism), one must be informed and participate in some form of mass communication.[206] On the other hand, digital political statements are often separated from actual organizing. Images of trauma can become disciplinary images that, paradoxically, paralyze self-activity. As the Locust Arts and Letters Collective (LALC) argues in "Socialist Irrealism vs. Capitalist Realism:"

---

204 This is not to say these are the same phenomena, but to point out the mutually reinforcing nature of what Friedrich Engels called "social murder" (which we see in the pandemic) and a conscious political exterminism (which we see in Israel's genocide in Gaza).

205 See Dean, Jodi, *Democracy and Other Neoliberal Fantasies: Communicative Capitalism and Left Politics* (Duke University Press, 2009) and Dean, Jodi, "Why the Net is not a Public Sphere," *Constellations* Volume 10, No. 1 (Blackwell Publishing, 2003).

206 I have taken this formulation of "war of position" vs. "war of maneuver" from Andreas Malm. Malm counterposes the war of position as a kind of misinterpretation of Gramsci (that might foster passivity) to a more active war of maneuver (informed by the politics of Leninism). See this following interview with Sebastian Bludgen, editor of *Historical Materialism*, "Andreas Malm on Palestine, Climate Activism and over-shooting 1.5 °C," Verso Books YouTube (November 23, 2023): https://www.youtube.com/watch?v=kVC8lL84UrU.

Videos of police brutality, racism, and violence, on the one hand "prove" the decades-long narratives of Black people, people of color, and the poor. The constantly mounting evidence had little impact on the capitalist state. But there is a secondary problem. Videos of police terror, because they are plucked from the larger metanarrative of a racist capitalism, *conceal* something. They conceal the *objective weakness* of the police. They conceal that, under conditions of solidarity and class consciousness, the police are vastly outnumbered by the class and by the specific groups they oppress. In this way, these videos act as disciplinary images. They give us, in part, an illusion of our weakness, an exaggeration of police power, while often retraumatizing the victims of the police. This is not to say we shouldn't record and document police racism and violence. We should. If only to try to protect the specific human beings they are attacking. Nevertheless, the way these images work in communicative capitalism is highly contradictory.[207]

What is called for is, in part, a democratic, collective and totalizing counter-imagination: a poetry and politics of a *reconstituting* — but not reductive — political and artistic subject.

CYBORGS IN CRISES

There is a proliferation of intensive existential material crises — climate change, the relative decline of western imperialism as expressed in Ukraine and Palestine, economic crises and immiseration, and the

---

207 Locust Review, "Socialist Irrealism vs. Capitalism Realism," *Red Wedge Magazine* (February 18, 2020): http://www.redwedgemagazine.com/online-issue/socialist-irrealism-vs-capitalist-realism.

growth of fascism and the far-right. These crises seem to dwarf the responsive capabilities of the existing left. This is accompanied by a seemingly uncontrolled overgrowth of what some Marxists call the cultural superstructure: an emphasis on discursiveness and individual performance on digital social media. While seemingly democratic in access, digital culture not only shifts the forms of specific artworks and political gestures, it is moreover structurally biased toward a kind of philosophic idealism (tending to separate cultural and political gestures from their organic constituencies and authenticities). What specifically is said — while still important — has become less determinant over time than the fact that something is being said.

Discrete forms of culture — the painting, photograph, film, poem — have come to mimic the neoliberal commodity and financial form. The memeing of culture and its reconstruction by Artificial Intelligence (AI) apes the digitized production and financial networks of contemporary capitalism. In this way the AI generated digital image is not unlike the collateralized debt obligations (CDOs) and similar financial instruments that enabled the global financial crisis in 2008. CDO's — comprising hundreds of thousands of "real life" mortgages — were compiled largely by computer programs. They became so complex that even their Wall Street creators had little idea as to what was in them.[208] Like their financial counterparts, digital images are today placed into a seemingly unknowable montage; or remixed into "new" discrete "Frankenstein" images by AI. The AI's digital montage has a meaning and

---

208 This was widely reported in the aftermath of the 2008 crisis and sketched in several dramatic films and documentaries. *Forbes* wrote the following in 2010: "CDOs are collateralized debt obligations. If you don't know what that is, you're not alone; no one on Wall Street seems to know what they are, either! PBS does a good job of explaining a CDO. A CDO is an 'investment-grade security backed by a pool of various other securities. CDOs can be made up of any type of debt, in the form of bonds or loans.'" See "Down the Rabbit Hole: Deciphering CDOs" (May 17, 2010): https://www.forbes.com/2010/05/17/what-are-collateralized-debt-obligations-personal-finance-cdos.html?sh=397608e32dc3.

aggregation that is, in the end, mostly shaped by the needs of capital. In the case of financial instruments this was to maximize the profitability of investments and discipline productive capital. The holy grail for digital finance, as Edemilson Paraná notes in *Digitalized Finance: Financial Capitalism and Informational Revolution*, is the eradication of latency (the delay in computer network communication). The digital memeification of finance, increasingly free from delay in human or computer-decision making, automates the best possible investment outcome. Capital flows where it is "needed" when it is "needed." Human intervention is minimized.[209] If the primary economic motivator of digital finance is capital accumulation, for social media it is engagement and information accumulation. This is the commodity that the social industry sells to the remainder of the capitalist class. However, both these phenomena — finance and digital culture — are overdetermined by immediate political economies and ideology. As noted, the social media industry is designed with a particular capitalist-utopian conception of the images and texts placed within it, a kind of separation of the cultural and material aspects of life. What is placed into the digital firmament seems to lose authenticity, context, and discrete meaning.

BARBENHEIMER

Digital gestures become transparent, to borrow from the poet Rodney Jones. They *seem* to float separately from material and political crises. But this is an illusion. A movie about atomic weapons is fused with a two-hour feminist toy advertisement creating the *Barbenheimer* memes. *Barbenheimer* "floated," however, above a US proxy war with Russia in Ukraine, a world on the verge of accelerating the ethnic cleansing of Palestine, a world in which abortion rights had just been suspended for millions, a world in which European and American "leftists" defended the use

---

209 Paraná, Edemilson, *Digitalized Finance: Financial Capitalism and Informational Revolution* (Haymarket Books, 2018).

of depleted uranium munitions against Russian imperialism in Ukraine. I am referring here, of course, to the *Barbenheimer* meme rather than the discrete meanings and juxtapositions of the films, *Oppenheimer* and *Barbie*, released on the same day in July 2023. It is not that the meanings of those two films are unimportant — a biographical film about a problematic scientist who was key to the development of the atomic bomb and a mainline feminist appropriation of the Barbie-toy (albeit under the aegis of the corporation that owns it). However, it is to contrast those two discrete meanings within a related but different participatory capitalist montage created in the digital gesamtkunstwerk of social media. While this clearly had marketing benefits for the movie studios, the meme was overdetermined by several cultural and structural factors and heavily conditioned by capitalist ideology. How do we read, in retrospect, the glossy fusion of "feminist Barbie" and scientific mass murder in light of the "diverse" Biden administration's support for racial genocide? Karine Jean-Pierre is the first openly gay person and first Black woman to serve as a presidential press secretary. On October 30th she compared Palestine solidarity protesters, many of whom are people of color and Jewish, to white supremacists. Symbolic reparations, in the form of political appointments from the neoliberal center appeared in real-time alongside new historic crimes. Material reparations were out of the question.[210]

The primacy of exchange-value has overcome use-value in mass media. In Marxist economics, use-value refers to the use of a commodity. Bread is for eating. Exchange-value refers to the money-value of the commodity in the market. Bread is for sale at the bakery. In capitalism, as Marx argued, commodities are produced primarily for exchange value.[211] However, even in capitalism, there have been partial exceptions. Because

---

210 It should be noted that the *Barbenheimer* meme could be read as polysemic. It is possible to read it as a critique of itself. However, it was not my experience in seeing these memes that criticality was frontloaded when these memes were shared — including from ostensibly radical persons.

211 See the first chapter of Marx, Karl, *Capital Volume 1* (Penguin Classics, 1992).

the ideological apparatus of the media was central to maintaining class rule, facilitating debates within the bourgeoisie,[212] and promoting certain conceptions of society, the state interfered with the media to direct its activities in a particular way, subsidizing or financing certain forms of media or proscribing its mandates and actions.[213] In communicative capitalism, what is being said is often less important than the fact something is being said. The more communication there is, the more information can be accumulated, which can be realized as profit in the market.

How is this experienced by most individuals? The volume of communication, in tandem with constant crises, seems to collapse time. Everything is happening everywhere all at once.[214] But the exploited and oppressed subject is still constrained by geography and time.

Climate change threatens to undermine the abundance necessary to create an equal and democratic post-capitalist society. Contemporary Marxists are engaged in a debate on "economic growth" — divided between those who argue economic growth is still possible and desirable versus those who argue that growth is no longer necessary to create socialism — that there is already more than enough "abundance" to allow for a post-capitalist society — and that further capital accumulation will compound metabolic rift, calling into question the viability of civilization itself.[215] This growth/degrowth debate overlaps (albeit not identi-

---

212 This is, after all, the original model for Jürgen Habermas' "Public Sphere" — the collective ideological apparatus of the British capitalist class.

213 See state media in Europe and the "Fairness Doctrine" in the US for example.

214 This is expressed in numerous films and books. See, for example, *Cloud Atlas* (the film and novel, 2012 and Septre, 2004), *Everything, Everywhere, All at Once* (2022), and the miniseries *Station Eleven* (2021) — based on the eponymous Emily St. John Mandel novel (Knopf, 2014)..

215 Malm seems agnostic on this debate. Metabolic rift is an eco-socialist concept popularized by John Bellamy Foster, based on his reading of Karl Marx's *Economic and Philosophic Manuscripts of 1844*. It refers to the gap between industrial consumption/production and nature's ability to recoup the materials used in that production/consumption. See Foster, John Belamy, "Marx's Theory of Metabolic Rift: Classical Foundations for Environmental Sociology," *American Journal of Sociology* Vol 105, No.

cally) with those who argue for a reconstitution of social democratic norms and those who argue for more revolutionary strategies. Andraes Malm has called for a "war communism" type mobilization to mitigate climate change — referring to the mass mobilization of the Bolsheviks from 1918-1920 to defend the October Revolution during the Russian Civil War.[216] More social democratic Marxists tend to argue that capitalism can produce growth and greater social spending while also minimizing climate change. Regardless of who is right (although I tend to agree with the degrowth argument) it seems clear that the ideologues of capital have decided (at least in the west) that growth and social policy are incompatible. Recent crises seem to indicate a ruling-class that is comfortable with large numbers of human beings, particularly those who are seen as surplus population, being written off.

AI threatens labor, recapitulating the dream of "cybernetic masters and robot slaves" that animates Silicon Valley ideology.[217] AI, in its capitalist iteration, threatens the subjectivity of art, while feeding back into the sense that subjectivity has been displaced more globally. AI image generators were initially marketed by their production of apocalyptic imagery. For example, in 2022, the Wonder AI Art Generator was promoted with apocalyptic images that had seemingly been prompted by the text "paint the last human selfie ever taken." The world is full of objects and images. What might have once represented God or human emancipation becomes digital wallpaper. The masses are denied the *substance* and *actuality* of subjective expression while at the same time given access to a *simulation* of subjective expression. The contemporary artist lives in a stalled teleology, a gothic-futurist relationship to cultural signs and gestures, floating in a world of often meaningless possibility.[218]

---

2 (September, 1999), 366-405. Available online here: https://johnbellamyfoster.org/wp-content/uploads/2014/07/Marxs-Theory-of-Metabolic-Rift.pdf

216 See Malm, Andreas, *How to Blow Up a Pipeline* (Verso, 2020) and Malm, Andreas, *Corona, Climate, Chronic Emergency: War Communism in the 21st Century* (Verso, 2020).

217 Barbrook and Cameron, "The Californian Ideology," 1-15.

218 This of course parallels a number of arguments made by Mark Fisher in *Capitalist*

THE SOCIAL-SUBJECTIVITY OF MARXISM

Marxism is, like the art of the hunter-gatherer, concerned with *both* individual and collective human subjects. This has been obscured by various determinisms. It has been, at the level of studying Marx himself, obscured by a divorce of the economic and philosophic — a marriage clearly expressed in the *Economic and Philosophic Manuscripts*. Marx describes the alienation of the worker as an alienation from "reality,"[219] in which the worker is — in the Lukácsian sense — reified or thingified. In pre-class societies, this labor is unalienated. The worker can imagine themself abstractly but has conscious control, or at least partial control (as part of a collective) over that abstraction. In class society, the worker becomes an unconscious object, while objects *seem* to become subjects. Marxism is, in this sense, a struggle to regain collective and individual subjectivity. It is a betrayal of Marxism when latter-day Marxists re-thingify the working-class as a political object sans agency. For Marx, alienated and exploited labor attenuated the worker from the "sensuous external world."[220] This alienation separates the worker from the *collective genius* of human species-being — the great leap forward in social knowledge that allowed for the creation of language, poetry, literature and art:

> Man [sic] is a species-being, not only because in practice and theory he adopts the species as his object (his own as well as those of other things), but — and this is only another way of expressing it — because he treats himself as the actual, living species, because he treats himself as a universal and therefore free being.[221]

Class society and capitalism with its intensive divisions of labor

---

Realism (Zero Books, 2009) and in other texts.

219 Marx, Karl, *The Economic and Philosophic Manuscripts of 1844* (Dover Books, 2007), 69.

220 Marx, *The Economic and Philosophic Manuscripts of 1844*, 70-73.

221 Marx, *The Economic and Philosophic Manuscripts of 1844*, 74.

estranges workers from that conscious being. From being a master of labor, the worker becomes an object of labor.[222] In this way, the contemporary memeification of culture and art, in the absence of social revolution, ratifies this alienation across all aspects of culture. Culture becomes, as a totality, alienated. Art becomes "text" and text becomes code. The machines make "paintings." You work at UPS. The machines write poetry. You work at Starbucks. The machines become actors. You are an adjunct professor. The machines make movies. The social ensemble is manifested in social labor and social media — but one's ability to shape it is obscured.

SOCIAL SUBLIME?

Social media, new fascisms, climate disaster, the decline of western imperialism — could all be described as "hyperobjects." According to Timothy Morton, hyperobjects are objects and phenomena which are "massively distributed in space-time" and therefore tend to overwhelm the distinctions needed for pattern discernment. Examples include climate change, black holes, relativity and oil spills. Morton gives the analogy of setting out to find the concept "animal" vs. a specific animal in a zoo, or to find "climate" as opposed to a specific instance of weather. He ties this to Marxist concepts as well as Martin Heidegger's idea of a "standing reserve" (*gestell*) — which Morton argues is central to Heidegger's notions of "technological violence." *Gestell* becomes a kind of object-revenge. The standing reserve of society turns on society. There are parallels with Georges Bataille argument that the economy produces an excess — an "accursed share" — beyond that which can be economically recuperable.[223] The wealth of society becomes an albatross

222 Marx, *The Economic and Philosophic Manuscripts of 1844,* 74-76.
223 Morton, Timothy, *Hyperobjects: Philosophy and Ecology after the End of the World* (University of Minnesota Press, 2013), Heidegger, Martin, *The Question Concerning Technology and Other Essays* (Harper, 1977), Heidegger, Martin, *Being and Time* (Harper, 2008), Bataille, Georges, *Visions of Excess: Selected Writings, 1927-1939* (University of Minnesota Press, 1985), Karl Marx, *Capital Volume 1* (Penguin Classics, 1992).

for the individual subject. The technological violence (in climate change or doom scrolling) follows you home from work.

For Morton, a hyperobject collapses foreground and background and unravels the Burkean sublime — in which the terror of subjective smallness gives the subject a renewed sense of mastery over other aspects of being — and the Marxist differentiation of subject and object. As noted, the most banal conversation (the weather) becomes either a denial of climate change or another apocalyptic moment in daily life. For Morton, apocalyptic art and films cease to be prophetic and have become a sort of apologetics. Hyperobjects defy subjective action because their "local manifestation," according to Morton, *is not* the hyperobject itself. Moreover, our moment of climate change is not climate change. Climate change stretches backwards in time for decades and forward in time for centuries.[224]

It should be noted that Morton roots his arguments in something called "object-oriented ontology." This has been criticized by many Marxists, including Andreas Malm. I suspect that Morton is, like many postmodernists and poststructuralists, describing a cultural phenomenon but over-naturalizing its conclusions. Object oriented ontology argues that objects can have agency. This observation *appears* true because of the overwhelming dominance of certain kinds of objects in our everyday lives — smartphones, for example. But these objects are shaped by human subjectivity and contested by class and other aspects of oppression. They do not have autonomy or true subjectivity and agency. At any rate, if hyperobjects seem to preclude or minimize individual and political subjectivity, there are concepts that hold out the chance of recouping subjectivity from large phenomena. For example, the aforementioned concept of the sublime.

For Edmund Burke, the nature of the sublime — the feeling of smallness in the face of overwhelming phenomena — pivots on *how*

---

224 Morton, *Hyperobjects,* 1-26.

it makes the subject feel small. The storm, mountain, symphony, may make the subject "small" but it does not displace subjectivity or obliterate it. Instead, it recasts other aspects of life. The storm is terrible and beautiful but it underlines that the more mundane aspects of life are malleable. You cannot change the storm, but you can change the more immediate parts of life. In this paradoxical way, the overwhelming objective character of the sublime invigorates subjectivity. There is arguably something of this sublime in the experience of a mass uprising, protest, or strike. The *individual* participant becomes *more* through their social collectivity. This sense of subjective empowerment, however, may falter in the face of something like climate change. Unlike a beautiful storm witnessed from a safe house — or an uprising witnessed from the solidarity of its collective center — you cannot weather climate change from a safe objective point.[225] The character of climate change reflects the potential hostility and alienation of Heidegger's "standing reserve," Marx's "dead labor," and Georges Bataille's "accursed share."

In Romantic art and poetry, the sublime was often considered "impossible" to capture. However, the *attempt* to capture this sublime was considered a kind of noble act or performance. See, for example, the landscape paintings of Caspar David Friedrich or the Hudson River School. Often read as a reaction against modernization and industry, the Romantics weren't necessarily against science or emancipatory politics, but the inhuman forms that science took, or the failures represented by the French Thermidor. See, for example, the enthusiasm Romantics such as William Blake, Francisco Goya, and Beethoven initially had for the French Revolution before their disillusionment during the Napoleonic Wars.

As noted, Georges Bataille argues that the economy produces an *excess* beyond what is economically recuperable. The artist Anupam Roy also notes this in terms of emotive-being (as a sort of by-product of

225 See Burke, Edmund, *A Philosophical Enquiry into the Origin of Our Ideas of the Sublime and Beautiful* (Anados Books, 2018).

the economic excess) that can either be directed toward something like socialism or something like fascism.[226] Material excess — what Batialle calls an 'accursed share' — is spent on luxury or war (what Marx and Engels called 'department III' of the economy in *Capital*),[227] or even spent on catastrophe more generally (for example, climate crisis as a result of the metabolic rift between nature and production).[228] What *would have been* ritual sacrifice in earlier forms of class society — to get rid of the "excess" wealth — is necessitated. However, in capitalism, this excess wealth threatens the system overall — as economic, political, social, and enviromental crises. The self-suicide of civilization becomes the 'sacrifice' of capitalism.[229]

In the 2010s, against postmodernism and vulgar Marxism, some Marxists around *Historical Materialism* and the journal *Red Wedge* began discussing the concept of *differentiated totality* (a non-reductive totality). I don't know who coined the term. I thought we had — I was an editor at *Red Wedge* throughout the 2010s — and then heard several other people use it independently. I had trouble finding it in print.[230] Rather than a fragmentary rhizomatic network we argued that an overall pattern of identities, exploitations, and oppressions was overdetermined by the conflict between capitalism and nascent class consciousness. A similar concept is outlined in Holly Lewis' comparative philosophy of

226 Turl, Adam interview with Roy, Anupam,. "We Are Broken Cogs in the Machine," *Red Wedge Magazine* (May 7, 2019): https://www.redwedgemagazine.com/online-issue/broken-cogs-in-the-machine.

227 Marx, Karl, *Capital Volume 3* (Penguin Classics, 1993).

228 See Foster, John Bellamy, *Marx's Ecology: Materialism and Nature* (Monthly Review Press, 2000), based in part on his readings of Marx, *Capital* Vol. 3.

229 Bataille, Georges, *Visions of Excess: Selected Writings, 1927-1939* (University of Minnesota Press, 1985).

230 Turl, Adam, "The Democratic Image," *Red Wedge Magazine* (April 19, 2016): https://www.redwedgemagazine.com/online-issue/democratic-image and Diaz, James, interview with Turl, Adam, "Interview with Artist Adam Turl," *Anti-Heroin Chic* (October 6, 2016) : https://heroinchic.weebly.com/blog/interview-with-artist-adam-turl.

queer theory, feminism and Marxism in *The Politics of Everybody*.[231] Because we found little on the concept of "differentiated totality" we borrowed a great deal from Mikhail Bakhtin's concept of the carnivalesque (and by extension Francois Rabelais).[232] The contemporary queer African-American left poet Richard Hamilton describes "differentiated totality" in their work as "discordant will."[233]

Importantly, differentiated totality, discordant will, and Anupam Roy's revised conception of excess,[234] occurs within the class as a whole, as well as in its particular segments and individuals. In Richard Hamilton's poem, "Object" — alternating between free verse and prose — he writes, recalling working as an AmeriCorps tutor in Atlanta:

> I almost never take the position that I know what is
> best for an individual. Watching that young man, I
> puzzled over factors that may have shaped his *discor-*
> *dant* will. Many students endured
>
> housing insecure
> arrangements
> with relatives
>
> in emergency shelters
>
> many more arrived at school
> having not
>
> eaten
> ravenous

231 Lewis, Holly, *The Politics of Everybody: Feminism, Queer Theory, and Marxism at the Intersection* (Zed Books, 2016).

232 Bakhtin, Mikhail, *Rabelais and His World* (Indiana Univserity Press, 1985).

233 See the *Locust Radio* interview with Hamilton, Richard, (hosts - Tish Turl, Laura Fair-Schulz, Adam Turl), "Richard Hamilton's Discordant Will," *Locust Radio* episode 10 (September 22, 2021): https://www.locustreview.com/locust-radio/locust-radio-ep-10-discordant-will.

234 Turl and Roy, "We Are Broken Cogs in the Machine."

for mediocre   school

lunch.
It was lunch.[235]

The implicit hope is that a class-conscious proletariat would be, in itself, not unlike Burke's storm, terrifying and beautiful while also *activating* the artistic and Marxist subject. Like the romantic sublime, or the exact forms of a truly democratic post-capitalist society in Marxism, this differentiated totality would not be easily mapped or deduced in form.[236]

THE CAPITALIST BOOK OF HOURS

The cybernetic is a contradiction between object and subject. Like Frankenstein's monster — and the working-class within capitalism— it has a potential to become *object revenge* — for the reified to become concrete, for object to become subject. It does this by struggling to be free. The working-class is the cybernetic subject, equally composed of living and dead labor. The collective-but-individuated performance of a dematerialized capitalism comes in contradiction with the lived experience of an increasingly cybernetic working-class. Social media has become a capitalist book of hours. Its promise of a world without material constraint stands in stark contrast to the constraint — including via its algorithms — in which the majority of the human race lives. The solace that the book of hours provides begins to wane.

As it does, the task of working-class artists is to create counter-imaginaries to the total art of capitalism. This includes the social performance that surrounds our work.

---

235 Hamilton, Richard, *Discordant* (Pittsburgh: Autumn House, 2023), 52.
236 Conceptions of discordant will/differentiated totality/excess(*modified) have inspired the editorial and design logic of *The Locust Review* (founded when Red Wedge was suspended in 2019/2020).

Western capitalism has outlived any sense of social development or progress. Culture has taken on an increasingly gothic hue. The ruins of an industrial heyday are illuminated by digital billboards. The cyber-utopianism of the early Internet has failed, exposing Silicon Valley's anti-democratic ideologies and economies. Social suffering goes unanswered by the political center, helping produce far-right governments and fascist movements. It is in this context that contemporary artists, as descendants of the modernist avant-gardes, have become institutionalized and weak, eschewing art's spiritual origins as well as modern art's emancipatory dreams. It is only by turning to the working class that we can salvage art's social and spiritual roots.

Only the working class can save us.

BIBLIOGRAPHY

Adkins, Brent, *Deleuze and Guattari's A Thousand Plateaus: A Critical Introduction and Guide* (Edinburgh University Press, 2015).

Adorno, Theodor, *Prisms* (MIT Press, 1983).

Antliff, Alan, *Anarchy and Art: From the Paris Commune to the Fall of the Berlin Wall* (Arsenal Pulp Press, 2007).

Badiou, Alain, *Rhapsody for the Theatre* (Verso, 2013).

Bakhtin, Mikhail, *Rabelais and His World* (Indiana University Press, 1984).

Baraka, Amiri, *SOS: Poems 1961-2013* (New York: Grove Press, 2014).

Barbrook, Richard, and Cameron, Andy, "The Californian Ideology," *Science as Culture*, Vol 6 (1996), 1-15.

Barlow, John Perry, "A Declaration of the Independence of Cyberspace," online paper (1996), distributed widely online in the 1990s, accessed here on March 10, 2022: https://www.eff.org/cyberspace-independence.

Bartelik, Marek, "Review: Beyond Belief," *Artforum* Vol 35, No 7 (March 1997), 97.

Bataille, Georges, *Visions of Excess: Selected Writings, 1927-1939* (University of Minnesota Press, 1985).

Benjamin, Ruha, *Race After Technology* (Polity Press, 2019).

Benjamin, Walter, "On the Concept of History" (1940), version at https://www.marxists.org/reference/archive/benjamin/1940/history.htm.

Benjamin, Walter, *The Work of Art in the Age of Its Technological Reproducibility and Other Writings on Media* (Harvard University Press, 2008).

Berger, John, *Ways of Seeing* (Penguin, 1972).

Bestley, Russ and Ogg, Alex, *The Art of Punk: The Illustrated History of*

Punk Rock Design (Voyageur Press, 2012).

Billet, Alexander *Shake the City: Experiments in Space and Time, Music and Crisis* (1968 Press, 2022).

Bishop, Claire, "Antagonism and Relational Aesthetics," *October* 110 (Fall 2004), 51-79.

Bishop, Claire, "Art of the Encounter: Antagonism and Relational Aesthetics," *Circa* No. 114 (Winter 2005), 32-35.

Bishop, Claire, *Artificial Hells: Participatory Art and the Politics of Spectatorship* (Verso, 2012).

Bishop, Claire, "Delegated Performance: Outsourcing Authenticity," *October* (Spring 2021), 91-112.

Bishop, Claire, *Installation Art* (Tate Publishing, 2005).

Bishop, Claire and Arguello, Gemma, "Towards a Philosophy of Installation Art," *Journal of Aesthetics and Art Criticism* 78 (3), 333-338.

Bogdanov, Alexander, "Immortality Day," in Groys, Boris, ed. *Russian Cosmism* (MIT Press, 2018), 215-228.

Bogdanov, Alexander, *Red Star: The First Bolshevik Utopia* (Indiana University Press, 1984).

Bourriaud, Nicolas, *Relational Aesthetics* (Paris: Les Presses Du Reel, 1998).

Breton, Andre, "The Automatic Message," *Minotaure* No. 3-4 (1933).

Buchloh, Benjamin H.D., "Raymond Pettibon: After Laughter," *October* 129 (Summer 2009), 13-50.

Burke, Edmund, *A Philosophical Enquiry into the Origin of Our Ideas of the Sublime and Beautiful* (Anados Books, 2018).

Cameron, Dan, Christov-Bakargiev, Carolyn, Coetzee, J.M., *William Kentridge* (Phaidon, 2010).

Campbell, Joseph, *The Masks of God Volume 1: Primitive Mythology* (Penguin, 1991).

Christov-Bakargiev, Carolyn, Lange, Christy, and Boubnova, Iara, *Nedko Solakov: All in Order, with Exceptions* (Hatje Cantz, 2011).

Cohen, Margaret, *Profane Illuminations* (University of Chicago Press, 1995).

Conley, Katharine, "Surrealism and Outsider Art: From the 'Automatic Message' to André Breton's Collection." *Yale French Studies*, no. 109 (2006), 129–143.

Corris, Michael, "Total Engagement: Moscow Conceptual Art: Schirn Kunsthalle, Frankfurt," *Art Monthly* Issue 319 (September, 2008), 18-20.

Cowie, Jefferson, *Staying Alive: The 1970s and the Last Days of the Working-Class* (New Press, 2010).

Cullinan, Nicholas, "From Vietnam to Fiat-nam: The Politics of Arte Povera," *October* 124 (Spring 2008), 8-30.

Cummings, Jordy, "I Know Who Else Was Transgressive: Teen Vogue Has Better Politics Than Angela Nagle," *Red Wedge Magazine* (August 2, 2017): http://www.redwedgemagazine.com/online-issue/nagle-review.

Danto, Arthur, *Unnatural Wonders*, (Colombia University Press, 2007).

Davies, David, "On the Very Idea of 'Outsider Art,'" *British Journal of Aesthetics* 49 (January 2009), 25-41.

Davis, Ben *9.5 Theses on Art and Class* (Haymarket Books, 2013).

Davis, Ben, "The Age of Semi-Post-Post-Modernism," *Artnet* (2016): http://www.artnet.com/magazineus/reviews/davis/semi-post-postmodernism5-15-10.asp.

Davis, Ben, *Art in the After-Culture* (Haymarket Books, 2022).

Davis, Ben, "A critique of social practice art," *International Socialist Review* (July 2013).

Dean, Jodi, *Democracy and Other Neoliberal Fantasies: Communicative Capitalism and Left Politics* (Duke University Press, 2009).

Dean, Jodi, "Why the Net is not a Public Sphere," *Constellations* Volume 10, No. 1 (Blackwell Publishing, 2003), 95-112.

Diaz, James interview with Turl, Adam, *Anti-Heroin Chic* (October 6, 2016): https://heroinchic.weebly.com/blog/interview-with-artist-adam-turl.

Dunn, Bill and Radice, Hugo, eds., *100 Years of Permanent Revolution: Results and Prospects* (Pluto Press, 2006).

Durant, Sam, *Black Panther: The Revolutionary Art of Emory Douglas* (Rizzoli, 2007).

Editorial (Turl, Adam and Billet, Alexander), "Art in (Corporate) America," *Red Wedge*, June 1, 2014).

Editorial, "Cyborgs! Shoot the Moon!," *Locust Review* 6 (Autumn 2021), 3-8.

Enright, Robert, "What Remains To Be Said: An Interview with Raymond Pettibon," *Border Crossings* Vol. 29 Issue 4 (December 2010), 20-35.

Fischer, Ernst, *The Necessity of Art* (Verso, 2010).

Fisher, Mark, *Capitalist Realism: Is There No Alternative* (Zero Books, 2009).

Fisher, Mark,"Exiting the Vampire Castle," *Open Democracy* (November 13, 2013). Available online: https://www.opendemocracy.net/en/opendemocracyuk/exiting-vampire-castle/.

Fisher, Mark, *Flatline Constructs* (Exmilitary, 2018).

Fisher, Mark,*K-Punk* (Repeater, 2018).

Foster, John Bellamy, *Marx's Ecology: Materialism and Nature* (Monthly Review Press, 2000).

Foster, John Belamy, "Marx's Theory of Metabolic Rift: Classical Foundations for Environmental Sociology," *American Journal of Sociology* Vol 105, No. 2 (September, 1999), 366-405. Available online here: https://johnbellamyfoster.org/wp-content/uploads/2014/07/Marxs-Theory-of-Metabolic-Rift.pdf.

Golumbia, David, *The Politics of Bitcoin: Software as Right-wing Extremism* (University of Minnesota Press, 2016).

Griffin, Allie, "NYC fruit vendor, 74, who sold banana devastated after it became viral $6.2M artwork: 'I am a poor man'," *New York Post* (November 28, 2024).

Groys, Boris, ed., *Russian Cosmism* (MIT Press, 2018).

Groys, Boris, "The Weak Universalism," *e-flux* 15, April 2010: http://www.e-flux.com/journal/the-weak-universalism/.

Groys, Boris, *The Total Art of Stalinism* (Verso, 2011).

Groys, Boris, and Kabakov, Ilya, *The Man Who Flew Into Space From His Apartment* (Afterall, 2006).

Hamilton, Richard, *Discordant* (Autumn House, 2023).

Harvey, David, *Rebel Cities* (Verso, 2019).

Heidegger, Martin, *Being and Time* (Harper, 2008).

Heidegger, Martin, *The Question Concerning Technology and Other Essays* (Harper, 1977).

Hoptman, Laura, *Beyond Belief: Contemporary Art from East-Central Europe* (Chicago: Museum of Contemporary Art, 1995).

Hoptman, Laura, *The Forever Now: Contemporary Painting in an Atemporal World* (New York: MoMA, 2015).

Juliff, Toby and Cox, Travis, "The Post-display Condition of Contemporary Computer Art," *emaj* 8 (April 2015), 4: https://emajartjournal.files.wordpress.com/2012/11/cox-and-juliff_the-post-display-condition-of-contemporary-computer-art.pdf.

Kabakov, Ilya, Tupitsyn, Margarita and Tupitsyn, Victor, "About Installation," *Art Journal* Vol. 58 No. 4 (Winter 1999), 62-73.

Kleeblatt, Norman L., et al, *Action/Abstraction* (Yale Press and the Jewish Museum, 2009).

Marcel Krenz, "Art in Times of Disaster," *Art Review* 53 (2002), 26.

Wendy Koenig, "The Heroic Generation: Fictional Socialist Realist Painters in the Work of Ilya Kabakov," *Southwestern Art Conference Review* Vol. 10 Issue 4 (2009), 448-455.

Ladendorf, Tom, "The Group of Artists That's Winning Fair Pay by Targeting Nonprofits," *In These Times*, January 26, 2016: http://inthesetimes.com/article/18764/wages-for-arts-sake.

Lefebvre, Henri, *The Production of Space* (Blackwell, 1991).

Lewis, Holly, *The Politics of Everybody: Feminism, Queer Theory, and Marxism at the Intersection* (Zed Books, 2016).

Lewis-Williams, David, *The Mind in the Cave* (Thames and Hudson, 2002).

Lewis-Williams, David, "Debating Rock Art: Myth and Ritual, Theories and Facts," *The South African Archeological Bulletin* Volume 61, No. 183 (June 2006), 105-114.

Lewis-Williams, David and Hodgson, Derek, "Shamanism, Phosphenes and Early Art: An Alternative Synthesis," *Current Anthropology* Volume 1, Number 5 (December 2000), 866-873.

Lippard, Lucy, *Six Years: The Dematerialization of the Art Object* (University of California Press, 1997).

Locust Review, "Socialist Irrealism vs. Capitalism Realism," *Red Wedge Magazine* (February 18, 2020): http://www.redwedgemagazine.com/online-issue/socialist-irrealism-vs-capitalist-realism.

Löwy, Michael, *Fire Alarm: Reading Walter Benjamin's 'On the Concept of History,'* (Verso, 2005).

Löwy, Michael, *Morning Star: Surrealism, Marxism, Anarchism, Situationism, Utopia* (Austin: University of Texas Press, 2009).

Löwy, Michael and Sayre, Robert, *Romanticism Against the Tide of Modernity* (Duke University Press, 2001).

Malm, Andre, *Corona, Climate, Chronic Emergency: War Communism in the 21st Century* (Verso, 2020).

Malm, Andreas, *How to Blow Up a Pipeline* (Verso, 2020).

Marx, Karl, *Capital Volume 1* (Penguin Classics, 1992).

Marx, Karl, *Capital Volume 3* (Penguin Classics, 1993).

Marx, Karl, *The Economic and Philosophic Manuscripts of 1844* (Dover, 2007).

Metcalf, Eugene W., "Black Art, Folk Art, and Social Control," *Winterthur Portfolio* Vol. 18 No. 4 (Winter 1983), 271-289.

Mihaylova, Vladiy, "Nedko Solakov and the Rest of the World" *Flash Art* 43 (January-February 2010).

Mitchell, Stanley, ed., Benjamin, Walter and Mitchell, Stanley, *Understanding Brecht* (Verso, 1977).

Morton, Timothy, *Hyperobjects: Philosophy and Ecology after the End of the World* (University of Minnesota Press, 2013).

Naiman, Eric, "When a Communist Writes Gothic: Aleksandra Kollontai and the Politics of Disgust," *Signs*, Vol. 22, No. 1 (Autumn, 1996), 1-29.

Nochlin, Linda, *Courbet* (Thames and Hudson: 2007).

Paraná, Edemilson, *Digitalized Finance: Financial Capitalism and Informational Revolution* (Haymarket Books, 2018).

Pohl, Rebecca, *An Analysis of Donna Haraway's Cyborg Manifesto* (Routledge/Macat, 2018).

Plant, Sadie, *The Most Radical Gesture: The Situationist International in a Post-Modern Age* (Routledge, 1992).

Radoschevich, Danica, "Zombie Gallery? The German Ideology and the White Cube," *Red Wedge* (February 8, 2015): http://red-wedgemagazine.com/commentary/the-white-cube-and-the-german-ideology-gallery-space-as-bourgeois-farce.

Rainer, Yvonne, "Yvonne Rainer Blasts Marina Abramović and MOCA LA," *The Performance Club* (November 11, 2011): https://theperformanceclub.org/yvonne-rainer-blasts-marina-abramovic-

and-moca-la/.

Raymond, Eric S., *The Cathedral and the Bazaar* (O'Reilly: 1999).

Resnikoff, Jason, *Labor's End: How the Promise of Automation Degraded Work* (University of Illinois Press, 2021).

Robinson, Walter, "Flipping and the rise of Zombie formalism," *ArtSpace* (April 3, 2014): https://artspace.com/magazine/contributors/see_here/the_rise_of_zombie_formalism-52184.

Schlegal, Amy Ingrid, "The Kabakov Phenomenon," *Art Journal* Vol. 58 No. 4 (Winter, 1999), 98-101.

Seymour, Richard, "Hegemony begins in the workplace," *Lenin's Tomb* (February 19, 2014): http://www.leninology.co.uk/2014/02/hegemony-begins-in-workplace.html.

Sholette, Gregory, *Dark Matter: Art and Politics in the Age of Enterprise Culture* (Pluto, 2011).

Schradie, Jen, *The Revolution That Wasn't: How Digital Activism Favors Conservatives* (Harvard University Press, 2019).

Stewart, Jack, *Graffiti Kings: New York City Mass Transit Art of the 1970s* (Melcher Media, 2009).

Turl, Adam, "Against Hopepunk," *Locust Review* (January 13, 2020): https://www.locustreview.com/blogs/against-hopepunk.

Turl, Adam, "Against the Weak Avant-Garde," *Red Wedge Magazine* (April 5, 2016): http://www.redwedgemagazine.com/online-issue/weak-avant-garde.

Turl, Adam, "The Democratic Image," *Red Wedge Magazine* (April 19, 2016): https://www.redwedgemagazine.com/online-issue/democratic-image.

Turl, Adam, "Interrupting Disbelief: Narrative Conceptualism and Anti-Capitalist Studio Art," *Red Wedge Magazine*, February 8, 2015.

Turl, Adam, "A Thousand Lost Worlds: Notes on Gothic Marxism," *Red Wedge* (old site, 2014).

Turl, Adam, "The Work of Art in the Age of Digital Reproduction," *Red Wedge Magazine* (May 1, 2019): http://www.redwedgemagazine.com/online-issue/digital-reproduction.

Turl, Adam interviews Roy, Anupam, "We Are Broken Cogs in the Machine," *Red Wedge Magazine* (May 7, 2019): https://www.redwedgemagazine.com/online-issue/broken-cogs-in-the-machine.

Turl, Adam, Turl, Tish, and Fair-Schulz, Laura interview Hamilton, Richard, "Richard Hamilton's Discordant Will," *Locust Radio* episode 10 (September 22, 2021): https://www.locustreview.com/locust-radio/locust-radio-ep-10-discordant-will.

Vidokle, Anton, "In Conversation with Ilya and Emilia Kabakov," *e-flux journal* #40 (December, 2012).

Wetzler, Rachel "How Modern Art Serves the Rich," *The New Republic* (February 26, 2018).

Whitley, David, *Cave Paintings and the Human Spirit* (Amherst, New York: Prometheus, 2009).

ACKNOWLEDGMENTS

A lot of folks helped me with this book. Many more shaped the articles, artworks, politics, and discussions that fed into it.

Most of all, I want to thank my partner and collaborator, Tish Turl, as well as all the current and former artists, writers, contributors and editors at both *Red Wedge Magazine* and *Locust Review* — Alexander Billet, Omnia Sol, Alice McIntyre, Jordy Cummings, Crystal Stella Becerril, Adam Marks, Leslie Lea, Anupam Roy, R. Faze, Labani Jangi, Adam Ray Adkins, Mike Linaweaver, Holly Lewis, Hope Asja, Jase Short, Danica Radoshevich, Jessica Allee, Ajith Nedumangad, Jason Netek, Keith Walsh, Laura Fair-Schulz, Drew Franzblau, Grant Mandarino, Nikeeta Slade, Brit Schulte, J. Matthew Camp, Richard Hamilton, Joe Sabatini, Cat Moir, and everyone else who worked on those projects. Not everyone is still with us, and some of us went in very different political or artistic directions, but I am always in your debt.

I want to thank Saman Sepheri, Sophie Hand, Patricio Fuentes, Brett Sperry, Bobby Quellos, Paul Mullan, James Helfrich, Glenn Allen, Noreen McNulty, Anna Maria Tucker, Kyle Preckwinkle, Ellie Soma, Frances Madeson, Terry Suhre, Mary Lee O'Hara, Deborah Tudor, Victor Ludwig, Paul Kirk-Davidoff, Matt Ashmore, Carrie Vine, Phil Gasper, Nick Shillingford, M.F., William Knight, Laura Borger, Judy Simpson, Dennis Fritz, Karen Burke, Luke Herron-Titus, and all those who have supported me and my partner's art practice over the years. This book is a direct result of that work.

I am also indebted to many brilliant instructors at both Southern Illinois University-Carbondale and Washington University in St. Louis — Najjar Abdul-Musawwir, Heather Bennett, Buzz Spector, Cinzia Padovani, Jyotsna Kapur, Wago Kreider, Mike Phillips, Joe Shapiro, Cade Bursell, Michael Byron, Haley Farthing, Erin Palmer, Angela Reinoehl, Travis Janssen, Monika Weiss, Patricia Olynyk, and many others. I also want to acknowledge my former colleagues at the University of Nevada - Las Vegas department of art. All of you helped me, directley or indirectly, with this text.

Bram E. Gieben and Mike Watson from Revol Press offered a great many productive suggestions and revisions to earlier drafts of this book. Mike Watson's support in making this book a reality was incalculable. My friend and neighbor, Craig Wilson, copy edited intermediate drafts of the manuscript. Of course, any remaining errors are mine and mine alone.

I am also obliged to recognize my comrades in Chicago, St. Louis, Las Vegas and Carbondale — and everywhere else — for grounding my work in the actual class struggle. In particular, I want to thank my comrades in the Carbondale Assmbly for Radical Equity (CARE), the Southern Illinois Democratic Socialists of America (SIDSA), and my many unaffiliated comrade-neighbors .

Last, but not least, I want to express my gratitude to my parents, Albert Turl and Vicky Turl, who have always been supportive, despite my apparent disinterest in mainstream ideas of success, and who taught me, perhaps not always intentionally, to look for pathos and beauty while trying to do the "right thing."

Until the world is ours.

— Adam Turl, Carbondale, Illinois, 2025

Revol Press aims to revive countercultural dreaming alongside incisive materialism, emphasizing quality over edgy content and hot takes, putting out considered yet incisive reflections in a timely manner. We pledge to support established writers and discover new talent, prioritizing fair royalties, ongoing dialogue, and an emphasis on quality essays and books that promote formal and theoretical innovation.

Our writers are part of a collective effort in publishing, not only making competitive royalties from their own books but taking a percentage of profits from all the books we produce and sell.

Revol is here to reassert the creative opposition of the author, in solidarity. Where once you paid lip service to the revolution and were considered credible, now you can build something revolutionary without compromise.

www.revolpress.com

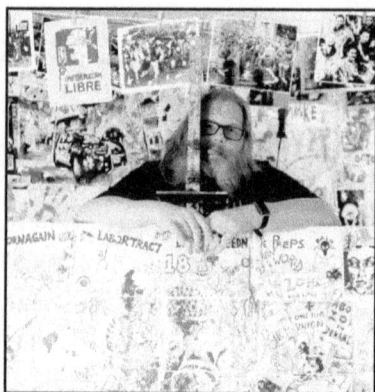

Adam Turl is an artist and writer in southern Illinois,
an editor at *Locust Review,* a member of the Locust
Arts and Letters Collective and the Southern
Illinois Democratic Socialists of America.
They work on an evolving art project and DIY
community organizing space, the *Born Again Labor
Museum*, with their partner, Tish Turl.

More praise for *Gothic Capitalism*...

This book is at once a protest and a clearing of the path forward. Adam Turl traces the paralysis of the art world, exacerbated by social media and AI, under neoliberalism and a rising far-right, and reclaims art in a profoundly Marxist sense — as a critique of existing conditions and the very human desire for transcendence, going back to the evolution of our species as cave painters.
— Jyotsna Kapur, author of *The Politics of Time and Youth in Brand India: Bargaining with Capital* (2013).

Drawing on the theory of uneven and combined development, Turl adumbrates what is gothic about contemporary capitalism and why it is experienced as such by the 'differentiated totality' of today's global proletariat: while we have been launched into a cybernetic and digital future, behind this future's techno-utopian promises lie only new modes of exploitation and domination and the uncanny, horrific return of archaic socio-economic violences.
— Joe Shapiro, author of *The Illiberal Imagination: Class and the Rise of the U.S. Novel* (2017).

www.ingramcontent.com/pod-product-compliance
Lightning Source LLC
Chambersburg PA
CBHW020710260425
25691CB00001B/3